weaving

A COMPLETE INTRODUCTION TO THE CRAFT OF WEAVING

INCLUDING PHOTOGRAPHS IN FULL COLOUR

Nell Znamierowski

DESIGNED BY AND PRODUCED UNDER
THE SUPERVISION OF WILLIAM AND SHIRLEY SAYLES

PAN BOOKS LTD : LONDON

FOREWORD

Here is a book that teaches weaving in an interesting, simple and direct manner. As a weaver myself, closely associated with textile design and with weavers in industry, I consider the beginner fortunate to be introduced to the world of handweaving by means of this instructive book.

Handweaving is fascinating to most people but attempted by relatively few, probably because it seems more complex than it is. As in all crafts, a basic interest is required before the first step towards instruction is taken. Once the decision has been made to pursue this rewarding craft, it is most important to obtain a proper background of fundamental knowledge. In this book, Nell Znamierowski has successfully projected all the essentials of handweaving, including an imaginative and contagious flair for pattern, texture, colour, and good taste.

A unique feature of this book is the presentation of step-by-step projects, including adaptations of designs which were stimulated by Nell Znamierowski's travels in Greece and Finland. Of particular interest is the valuable information she has provided on how to dye yarns.

There are many more dividends in this book that you will discover for yourself.

This is good reading and good weaving.

BOB CARR

First British edition published 1973 by Pan Books Ltd,
33 Tothill Street, London, SW1.
2nd printing 1976
ISBN 0 330 23561 3
© 1967 by Western Publishing Company, Inc

PRINTED IN ENGLAND BY CRIPPLEGATE PRINTING CO LTD LONDON & EDENBRIDGE

contents

acknowledgement

Among those who have assisted in the preparation
of this book, special thanks are due to:

Hal Halverstadt, *Consultant*
Betty MacDonald, *Design*
Louis Mervar, *Photography*
John Giannoni, *Artist*
Olivia Buehl, *Picture Research*

Poncho shirt, 72 × 65 cm (28¼ × 25½ in.) from Middle Paracas Culture (*c* 600 BC) of Peru, woven in tapestry technique of alpaca wool. (Collection of the Textile Museum, Washington, DC; photo courtesy Museum of Primitive Art, New York)

INTRODUCTION

Weaving can be defined simply as the interlacing of threads at right angles to form a web or fabric. However, it is much more than this in terms of the excitement and satisfaction that you will find in the actual process of creating a fabric.

This book is written for the new weaver who has access to a floor or table loom and for the potential weaver who has not yet decided whether to invest in a loom. The construction of a simple frame loom, as described in this book, offers the latter a means with which to be initiated into this fascinating craft.

The workings of a handloom and the mechanics of handweaving are easily mastered with a little guidance, encouragement and application. This book, I hope, will give you the guidance and encouragement. The application will come as you find yourself becoming more and more devoted to this craft.

(*Above*) Woman of old Peru weaving on a horizontal backstrap loom, from sixteenth century drawing. (Courtesy the Smithsonian Institution)
(*Below*) Man weaving on an upright 2-shaft counter-balanced loom, from Mendel's Twelve Brothers Manuscript, 1527. (Courtesy The Bettmann Archive)

THE HISTORY OF WEAVING

When we become weavers, our efforts form part of the modern link in the long chain of weaving history that dates back 20,000 years or more. It is thought that early man first used the weaving process by criss-crossing and intertwining twigs, reeds, and rushes. Later, as he became acquainted with other fibres and animal hairs, he employed these also in his rough works.

Throughout the centuries of evolution that followed, the spindle and the loom were developed – the former in the attempts to obtain a longer continuous thread from the fibres and animal hairs, and the latter as a stable fixture on which to attach these threads. Types of looms varied from area to area rather than from century to century. The ancient Greeks seemed to prefer the same type of upright loom, on which one weaves from the top down, as did some North American Indian tribes and the early Scandinavians. Egyptian weavers of about 2500 BC used another type of upright, or vertical, loom similar to that of the later Persians, and also a horizontal loom, such as was used by the Incas and is still used today in Mexico, Guatemala and Peru. Whatever loom was employed, the principle remained the same – passing and interlocking a weft, or horizontal thread, through a stationary warp, or vertical threads.

Although fabrics of the utmost beauty and sheerness were woven even in the days of the ancients, weaving tools and supplies were in a constant process of refinement in order to enhance further the finished product. Europe, until the time of the early Renaissance, depended on traders and Crusaders to bring her the elaborate textiles from the Far and Near East. Then the Italian weavers mastered the intricate weaves and skills of the Orient, as did eventually the French, Spanish and English, so that they could make their own velvets, damasks and brocades.

In 18th-century England the drive for increased textile production and ease of operation was continually going on and led eventually to the discoveries that brought about the Industrial Revolution. However, when the first settlers came to America, they had no need of such elegant fabrics and concentrated their labours on plain goods for the simple household and clothing demands of the times.

Research and invention are still an important part of the weaving industry. Some of the new equipment and processes are vastly intricate and complicated but, as you become more familiar with handweaving, you will see that the basic techniques remain the same, whether done on a handloom or a high-speed power loom.

WHY WEAVE?

Although I regard all weaving as allied to the arts, and there are those of you who will want to use it only as a means of self-expression to create beautiful tapestries and wall hangings, weaving also has a very practical side. A purse can be as much an object of beauty as a wall hanging, and the wall hanging as useful as the purse, since it adorns a space that otherwise might be barren. Neither is more lovely than the other and neither is more important to weave.

Smaller items such as handbags, cushion covers, stoles and table mats are all useful accessories and make wonderful gifts. There is nothing more pleasant for the giver or receiver than a present made with someone especially in mind. The practical aspect of weaving sometimes can be put to profit, for every year there are more craft shops and fairs springing up around the country. These outlets specialize in selling handwoven items, so perhaps this is your chance to earn some 'pin' money.

For those battling with an illness, weaving can be a help on the road to rehabilitation. It is a craft long known for its therapeutic value and is becoming increasingly popular in many hospitals.

It is a craft for young and old. As long as the loom is simple and the yarn fairly strong, children are fascinated by weaving and take great pride in the end result. I still remember making potholders on my first simple frame loom when I was eight or nine years old.

As with all crafts, a certain amount of patience is required, but patience will grow and relaxation settle in as you build up your skills and become intrigued with the interplay of colour, the texture of yarns, and the beauty and logic of fabric construction. Unless you are weaving to a deadline, whether you are slow or fast does not matter. What does

A simple early Peruvian loom showing a portion of a tapestry band. (Courtesy The American Museum of Natural History)

'Cottleston Pie' tapestry, 58 × 66 cm (23 × 26 in.), woven of wool, silk, rayon and cotton by Pamela Stearns. (Research files of the American Craftsmen's Council)

matter is the amount of enjoyment and fascination you find in the delight of 'doing'. This 'doing' is a constantly revitalizing process for, as you watch the woven article develop on your loom, new ideas and endless possibilities for further exploration open up before you.

THE WEAVING PROCESS AND THE HANDLOOM

A fabric, whether it is a rug, tapestry or suiting material, is made up of a warp and a weft. The warp consists of the lengthwise threads, also called ends. When fabric is held up in front of us, these are the vertical threads. It is this warp that will be interlaced with the filling threads, also called weft. In order to accomplish this interlacing without difficulty and to give pleasing results, the warp is put on a loom in a manner that gives the warp ends even tension.

We all know what darning looks like and how it is achieved by going over and under threads with a needle. Plain weaving is like darning – but without the needle. In place of the needle, a shuttle is used. In weaving, the 'over' ends are lifted first while the 'under' ends remain stationary. The weft goes through the opening between them. This opening is called the shed. It allows the shuttle, which carries the weft thread, to glide smoothly between the warp ends. These ends are lifted by various means according to the type of loom you have. By repeating this process of lifting a set of ends, passing the weft through and beating it down into position, you are weaving.

Looms may be of many types, but the basic techniques of weaving remain the same. Shown below is a small table model 2-shaft loom

The loom is the essential commodity in weaving, for there must be a place to stretch the warp. You will also need a few other tools, some of which can be improvised.

In order to have the warp properly on the loom, there are a few necessary preparatory steps. These include making the warp to the desired width and length on a warping reel or warping board. After the warp is completed it is made into a long chain and transferred to the loom. Here it is rolled onto the warp beam of the loom and then threaded through the heddles and reed. The heddles look like long needles, with the eye of the heddle found in the centre. They are attached to the shafts, the raising or lowering of which gives us the shed. The reed is in the front of the loom. It spaces the warp and beats down the weft.

To complete our preparation, the warp is tied to a front bar of the loom and bobbins are wound and placed in the shuttles. We can then begin weaving.

PLANNING YOUR WOVEN PROJECT

As you become involved with weaving, you will want to plan your own fabrics and woven articles. To aid you in this there are chapters on yarns and colour. A working knowledge of the various types of yarns and fibres will guide you in selecting the proper threads in the correct amounts for your planned project.

Colour selection and coordination are some of the most pleasurable aspects of weaving and give wide opportunity for your personality really to shine through. However, for those of you who feel a little hesitant or in need of guidance, I have included my own particular methods on how to use colour to its fullest advantage. Very often dealing with colour brings you to the point of wanting to dye your own shades. This in itself can be a very good exercise in getting to know colour and its properties intimately.

Along with choosing your own yarns and colours, you will want to pick out or develop the weave that suits your fabric best. Selecting the weave, the correct threading and the order in which the shafts will be raised for the shed openings are all part of the creativeness of weaving. They can best be understood and accomplished by learning how to draft weaves on graph paper. I have given the method I usually use, but in time you will develop your own. Drafting will also help you to understand fabrics already woven.

A LOOM TO MAKE

A very simple loom can be made at home out of a picture frame or a wooden stretcher such as artists use to stretch canvas. It is light,

Purse woven in plain weave with a finger-manipulated lace technique (see Lace Weaves, pages 74–9)

sturdy and portable and can be used to make rugs, tapestries, purses and other useful items.

Working on the frame loom will develop a feeling for the weaving process and, in the meantime, thought can be given to exactly the type of work you want to do and what kind of loom you should ultimately buy.

The frame loom can also serve as a second loom for those who have access to a larger one. Once you begin weaving, you will have so many ideas that you want to try out that a single loom may not be enough. It is quite common for weavers to work on more than one project at the same time. But keep in mind that the frame loom is used for 2-shaft or finger-manipulated weaves only.

There is a special method of preparing the warp and of weaving on the frame loom, but the principle of interlacing a warp and weft to form a fabric remains the same.

WHAT TO WEAVE

There are so many things to weave and so many different techniques to try that it is often difficult for a beginner to choose the right one as his first work. I have included projects that I feel will give the new weaver a good introduction to the workings of the loom and the possibilities of the woven craft. The first five projects are designed to be woven on either a frame loom or a table or floor loom. The remaining projects are exclusively for a 4-shaft table or floor loom, since I hope that eventually you will want to know and experience the pleasure of working on a loom that will allow you to do more complex structures.

None of the projects have to be followed exactly for, as you begin to feel at home at the loom, you will start to have your own ideas of what you want to explore. I find it a great asset to keep a small notebook handy. In it I jot down colour schemes or inspirations for patterns and attach interesting pieces of yarn that I want to try out.

I am a firm believer in sample warps in which you can experiment to your heart's content – and then use the fruits of your experience in your finished piece.

At the conclusion of the book there is a glossary for quick reference and a list of suppliers for looms, yarns, and other equipment. Your experiences in weaving will be, I trust, happy ones so that you will want to go on and broaden your knowledge; the list of books on page 95 is included for this purpose.

The frame loom (*above*) was used to make a section of a rya rug (*below*). Instructions to make this simple loom are on pages 16–17. For the rya rug directions, see pages 60–65

LOOMS

A loom is a device that holds the warp ends, or threads, taut so that a shed, or opening, can be formed. Through this shed the filling, or weft, is passed and the interlacing process between warp and weft achieved.

There are simple looms and complex looms. There are rough looms made of tree branches or scrap wood and sleek looms made of the best timber available. But they all must have a shed in order to weave. The way the shed is formed divides all looms into three basic categories.

LOOM BUYING

All the looms mentioned are equally serviceable and the kind you decide to buy depends purely on personal preference and on what you want to weave. If you want to concentrate on tapestries, shaft looms are superfluous. If you are interested in rugs and simple fabrics, nothing over 4 shafts is needed.

For scarves, table mats, and purses, a 69-cm (27-in.) loom is more than ample. The cost of the loom is determined by the materials used in making it, the workmanship involved, the width of the loom, and the number of shafts. Supply sources are listed at the end of this book.

FRAME, UPRIGHT OR VERTICAL, STICK OR BACKSTRAP LOOMS

These are variations of the same type of loom that has no shafts but has two different shed openings and at least one shed has to be opened by using a shed stick. In some cases, the fingers are used to open the space between two sets of warp ends. Since the fingers are used in our frame loom, this method will be discussed later.

These looms were at one time the only kind of looms, and all others developed from them. In the vertical loom, the warp faces the weaver in an up and down position. Tapestry looms are usually of this type. Backstrap and stick looms, which are primitive looms still used in many parts of Central,

FRAME LOOM

In the frame loom, the shed stick is turned on edge to form the first shed

TAPESTRY LOOM

Upright loom, for making rugs and tapestries. The wing nuts on top of the loom are used to maintain tension

South and North America, are horizontal looms, with the warp running back to front. Frame looms can be either vertical or horizontal, depending on whether they are attached to legs or supports or held in the weaver's lap.

These looms are the slowest to manipulate, but this does not mean that the results are less handsome. The ancient Incas wove on such looms and their fabrics have yet to be surpassed in beauty or technical skill.

TABLE LOOMS

Table looms can have a number of shed openings. The number depends upon the number of shafts, with the usual range from 2 to 16. The hand is the force that changes and opens the sheds. It does so by pressing on levers, turning knobs, or rotating wheels which in turn raise the shafts that have the warp strung on them through heddles.

Most table looms come in weaving widths from 20 to 81 cm (8 to 32 in.) and are easily transported and stored.

4-shaft rising shed table loom. The sheds are opened by pressing on the levers at the side of the loom

FLOOR LOOMS

The sheds are made by pressing on foot-controlled treadles, which leaves the hands free to throw and catch the shuttle. These looms are the fastest and most rhythmic of all to operate. They sometimes come with as many as 24 shafts or as few as 2; 16 is the normal maximum. In this book, we will not be concerned with looms of more than 4 shafts. The treadles are attached in the under part of the loom to slats of wood called lams. These lams then attach to the shafts. Pressing on the treadle pulls down on the lam which then either raises or lowers the shaft. If it is raised, this is called a rising shed. If it is lowered, the term is sinking shed. Jack type looms are common examples of the former, and counterbalanced looms of the latter. These looms come in weaving widths from 51 to 152 cm (20 to 60 in.).

You may possibly come across a countermarch loom, in which the shed operates on both systems at the same time; that is, one set of threads rises as the other sinks.

TABLE LOOM

FLOOR LOOM

4-shaft wooden floor loom with a rising shed. The sheds are made by pressing on the treadles

SHED STICK

HEDDLE ROD

HEDDLES

WARP

WARP-END BAR

TENSION STICK

SETT MARKS

FRAME LOOM

TAPESTRY LOOM

PARTS OF THE LOOM

In order to understand weaving, it is important to know the different parts of the loom. Here, illustrated and explained, are the parts of the frame and upright models.

Frame and Upright Models

In the frame loom the top of the frame serves as the back beam and the bottom as the breast beam. There are no shafts, treadles, levers, beater or reed.

Heddles Long loops of string through which the warp passes. They are attached to the heddle rod.
Heddle rod Carries the heddle loops and can be stationary or movable. Here it is stationary.
Sett marks Grooves filed or sawed into the top and bottom frames at 12·5-mm ($\frac{1}{2}$-in.) intervals. They take the place of the reed in the table and floor looms. The warp is spaced between them.

Shed stick A shed opening is made by turning this stick at a right angle to the warp. It is not attached to the loom.
Warp-end bar The warp ends revolve around this dowel rod to which are tied the beginning and end of the warp. It is placed at the back of the loom.
Tension stick Keeps the warp under proper tension for weaving. It is removed as the warp tightens in the process of weaving.
Tapestry comb Used to beat in the weft. An ordinary comb or fork may be used.

Here, illustrated and explained, are the parts of the table and floor models which, with few exceptions, are the same for both types.

Table and Floor Models

The list reads from the back of the loom to the front.

Warp beam The rotating lower back beam over which

CASTLE
SHAFTS
HEDDLES
LEVERS
BEATER
REED
BACK BEAM
OR SLABSTOCK
WARP
BEAM
RATCHETS
BREAST BEAM
CLOTH BEAM

BACK BEAM OR SLABSTOCK
WARP BEAM
TREADLES

TABLE LOOM   FLOOR LOOM

the unwoven warp is wound and stored.

Apron bars (not shown) The warp is tied to, or slipped over, the back apron bar. The beginning of the warp is tied to an identical bar at the front.

Apron (not shown) Attaches the apron bar to either warp beam in back or cloth beam in front.

Rachets Wheels with teeth to maintain the proper tension. One is at the back of the loom and one at the front.

Back beam or **slabstock** Provides a surface for the warp to glide over and helps to keep the warp at an even tension.

Castle The central main structure of the loom that houses the shafts.

Shafts Two horizontal bars between which the heddles are strung.

Heddles Lengths of metal, wire or string that are suspended between the shafts. They have a centre loop, or eye, through which the warp yarn passes.

Levers Located in the upper part of the castle on table looms and attached to the shafts. Working

them lifts the desired shafts. In some looms, knobs or wheels perform the same function.

Beater With the reed inserted in it, it beats the weft down.

Reed Comblike device inserted in the beater. It spaces the warp, in slots called dents, according to the width and density that is called for in the finished fabric. Reeds come in various sizes. The size indicates the number of dents per centimetre and is engraved in the first metal bar on the short side of the reed.

Breast beam Provides a foundation for the woven web as it moves down to the cloth beam.

Cloth beam Rolls up the finished cloth as it is woven off.

Treadles Foot pedals that operate shafts when pressed.

Lams (not shown) Levers lying between the treadles and shafts and attached to both. Pressing on a treadle pulls on the lams. This in turn raises or lowers the shaft to which each lam is attached.

SHED NO 1

Shed stick at top of frame loom is placed at a right angle to the warp to form the first shed. Tension stick, taped to front of loom, is removed as weaving progresses

Side view of first shed

SHED NO 2

Second shed is made by pulling on string heddles

Side view of second shed

(1) Unwoven warp wound on warp beam travels through **(2)** heddles on shafts, **(3)** through the reed in the beater. **(4)** Shuttle with weft passes through the successive sheds, and weaves cloth. **(5)** Woven cloth is stored on cloth beam at front of loom. The shafts move up and down forming the sheds. The beater moves back and forth beating the weft down

The Frame Loom

In order to open a shed on the frame loom, the shed stick is turned on edge at a right angle to the warp. From the side, the shed is seen to have a V-shaped passage. The shuttle carries the weft thread through this passage. The shed is closed by returning the shed stick to its original position, and the weft is beaten down with a comb or fork.

The next shed is made by pulling out and up on the string heddles. The weft is reinserted, the shed released, and the weft beaten down again.

As more and more cloth is woven, the shed openings become smaller and additional warp must be made available. One of the front tension sticks is then removed, and the warp-end bar pushed up so that the woven warp revolves around the bottom and up the back of the loom. Weaving is then continued.

Side view of woven cloth
revolving to back of loom

The Table or Floor Loom

The shed is formed by pressing on the treadles, or levers. On a floor loom the treadles are attached to the shaft *via* the lams in the order corresponding to the related sheds. The shuttle glides through the shed with the weaver leaving the thread at a diagonal.

The top of the beater is grasped firmly in the centre and pulled forward to beat down the weft. The beater is returned to its original position, the next shed is formed, and the weft beaten down once more. The shuttle is then passed through again.

When more warp is needed in front of the beater, the back ratchet is released. The woven warp is then revolved around the cloth beam until unwoven warp is brought into the weaving position. The back ratchet is resecured so that tension is held once more.

Weaving continues in this rhythmic manner – the shafts moving up and down and the beater backwards and forwards.

JOIN STRETCHER SIDES
AT RIGHT ANGLES

ATTACH METAL BRACKETS
AFFIX DOWEL ENDS
TO BRACKETS

11.4 cm (4½ in)

14.6 cm (5¾ in)

50.8 cm (20 in)

40.6 cm (16 in)

INSERT WOODEN PEGS
BRACE CORNER IN BACK OF FRAME

SAW OR FILE SHALLOW NOTCHES
ON TOP AND BOTTOM OF FRAME

CONSTRUCTION OF
THE FRAME LOOM

The frame loom used in this book for the first five projects was made of a wooden stretcher such as artists use to stretch canvas. This, plus the other materials, brought the cost of the loom to about £1. If scrap lumber is used, then a whole loom can be constructed for only the cost of the metal corner brackets, screws and bolts. A sturdy picture frame makes a good loom also.

In order to have the loom easily portable, the size was kept at 41 × 51 cm (16 × 20 in.). But it can be much larger and it can have legs. If a larger size than 61 × 71 cm (24 × 28 in.) is desired, then the loom should be made of hard wood at least 2·5 cm (1 in.) thick and 6 cm (2½ in.) wide. Otherwise, the frame will be too flimsy for the additional tension of a wider and longer warp.

Materials Needed

For the frame 4 stretcher sides (or strips) – 2 sides 41 cm (16 in.) long and 2 sides 51 cm (20 in.) long. These sides come from 21 to 91 cm (8 to 36 in.) and are prepared for joining. If scrap lumber is used for this size frame, it should be of hard wood, 19 mm (¾ in.) thick, 44·5 mm (1¾ in.) wide, and the same lengths as above.

For the heddle rod 2 63·5-mm (2½-in.) metal corner brackets with screws to attach to the frame.
1 wooden dowel rod at least 12·5 mm (½ in.) in diameter and as long as the width of the loom.
2 wood screws with self-locking nuts to attach the heddle rod to the corner brackets.

For the warp-end bar 1 wooden dowel rod at least 12·55 mm (½ in.) in diameter. The length can be the same as the width of the loom or up to 10 cm (4 in.) shorter.

For the shed stick 1 flat piece of wood 7·5 to 10 cm (3 to 4 in.) longer than the width of the loom, 9·5 mm (⅜ in.) thick in the centre, and 38 mm (1½ in.) wide. Since it will endure stress, the wood used must be very hard and sturdy. The long edges should be sandpapered until they are rounded and smooth. No sharp edge should remain to cut the warp ends as the sheds are made.

For the tension stick 1 or 2 thin, flat pieces of wood or extra heavy cardboard the width of the warp.

Tools needed Hammer, wood drill, screwdriver, saw and sandpaper.

Steps in Construction

1. If the stretcher is used, join its four sides at right angles by inserting the projections into the ready-made grooves. Insert the triangular wooden pegs that come with the stretcher sides into the inner corners of the frame and pound in firmly. If you have difficulty keeping the frame in position and maintaining the right angle, use a brace device as shown.

If scrap lumber is used, first saw the wood into the needed lengths and widths. Sandpaper any rough edges on which the yarn might catch, and smooth the corners. Lay the two short sides *on* the long sides at the corners and attach them with wood screws that will go through two thicknesses of wood. Two or three screws at each corner will be enough to hold the frame firmly in place. You can do an even better job if you put washers under the screw heads and a nut, or self-locking nut, where the screw exits from the back of the frame. If the screw protrudes from the nut, tape over it so that it will not scratch or mar the furniture.

Remember that you weave in just the open space between the side supports so that if you make a loom that is 41 cm (16 in.) wide, the weaving width will be actually 30·5 cm (12 in.). This is enough width to weave the projects in this book.

2. Bore two small holes on either side of the loom, four in all. The top holes should be 11·5 cm (4½ in.) from the top edge and the bottom holes 14·6 cm (5¾ in.) from the top edge. These distances are based on the 50·75 cm (20 in.) high loom. If you are going to make a larger loom, the bottom hole should be down about a third of the length of the entire loom. The holes are for the screws that attach the metal corner brackets to the loom. The brackets are at right angles to the frame. Onto this, the first dowel rod is attached.

3. Place the end of the first dowel rod over the hole at the tip of the metal bracket. Mark the dowel where it touches the hole and bore a hole through the dowel end. Repeat this at the other end. Place the rod onto the brackets again and affix with the screws. Attach a self-locking nut to the screws where they come through the rod and bracket. This is the heddle rod and in time will have string heddles attached to it.

4. Saw or file shallow notches on the top and bottom of the loom. These notches, or grooves, should be spaced 12·5 mm (½ in.) apart and extended across the entire width, starting 51 mm (2 in.) from both edges.

5. The warp-end bar, tension sticks and the shed stick are inserted when the warp is wound around the loom. The heddles are made at that time also.

About the Warp

The diagram of the frame loom on the opposite page illustrates how the loom should look when warped, or threaded. For complete warping instructions for the frame loom, see pages 38–9.

COLOUR WHEEL

COLOUR

Colour is one of the most appealing features of weaving and, to many, one of the most challenging. A colour can change according to quantity used, quality (texture or finish) of the yarn, and the surrounding colours of warp and weft.

Segments of two rugs of identical design, showing how designs are influenced by a change in colour

COLOUR VOCABULARY

All colours have the following characteristics:

Hue The pure colour and name of family in the spectrum it belongs to. Red is a pure colour; pink, rose, crimson, and wine belong to the red family.

Value The amount of lightness or darkness in a hue. The hue remains the same, but with the addition of white or black the value changes. Pink is a light value of red; wine a dark value.

Intensity The brightness or dullness of a colour. Again, hue is retained but the closer the colour comes to the pure hue, the brighter it is; the further away, the duller it is.

Colours are classified according to their positions on a colour wheel as shown:

Primary The pure colours from which all others derive. Red, yellow, and blue.

Secondary The colours that lie between the primaries, made by mixing two primaries. Orange, violet, green.

Tertiary The colours made by combining adjacent primaries and secondaries. Yellow-orange, red-orange, red-violet, blue-violet, blue-green, yellow-green.

Complementary The colours opposite each other on the wheel. Red is the complement of green, blue of orange, etc. If you mix two complementary colours of equal intensity, grey results. Mixing a hue with a little of its complement dulls its intensity.

Tint Blending hue with white.

Shade Blending hue with black.

Tone Blending hue with grey (black and white).

Besides the three principal characteristics of colour – hue, value, intensity – every colour falls into one of seven categories – pure hue, black, white, grey, tint, shade, tone. For example, a pale blue is a mixture of a blue hue with white and is called a tint. It also has a certain amount of value and intensity depending upon the amount of white and how far the resulting colour is removed from the original hue. When you look at colours, try to fit them into the correct category, to really see what makes up each colour.

In choosing your colours, you will find they form a colour scheme that fits into one of these harmonies:

Monochromatic Two or more values of one hue.
Analogous Combination of neighbouring colours on colour wheel.
Contrast Combination of complements or near-complements. Their intensity can be almost the same or vary greatly.

SOME COLOUR GUIDEPOSTS

1. When deciding upon colours, consider where the finished work will be used and with what other colours it will be seen. Twist the colours together to see the effect, or wind yarn around strips of white paper to simulate the warp. Then interweave the weft colours. These tests show how colours reflect each other's hue and change character when placed together.

2. Colour can be heavy, bright, light, sharp or delicate. Reds, oranges, and yellows can be warm and exciting; blues, violets and greens cool and calming. White with a colour makes the colour look deeper and darker even though the overall effect may be light. Black gives the colour a lighter and more brilliant look.

3. Neighbouring colours on the wheel subtract their common colour from each other. For example, in a green and turquoise combination, the green looks more like yellow-green since the blue in it combines visually with the blue in the turquoise. The same green next to lime will have a bluish-green hue since the yellow in it combines with the yellow in the lime.

4. When using several colours of great intensity, the brightest will appear even brighter, and the least bright almost dull, even though it may have looked bright by itself. If you want bright colours, but not an overall bright 'look', weave in enough neutral or dull colours to diminish the intensity of the bright ones.

5. In a rug, tapestry or wall hanging an area of great darkness can be created by placing it next to a very light area. Bright areas next to dark ones make the bright brighter, the dark darker. Keep in mind when making stripes or plaids that equal amounts of a light or dark colour make the light appear larger, the dark smaller. Warm colours also appear larger if combined with equal amounts of cool colours.

6. Complements can give very dramatic effects.

When of the same intensity, they clash, but by changing the weave or by reducing the amount or intensity of one colour, you get a less vibrant combination. A colour and its complement, used in the right proportion, will retain that colour closest to its original hue because the colour does not borrow from or reflect the complement but fights with it for prominence. Neutrals also bring forth a colour in its truest hue.

7. Two yarns of different hues could be combined to give the impression of a third hue. A red yarn and a blue yarn will give a purplish effect. Yarn texture will affect colour. A fuzzy mohair in the same colour as a gleaming smooth rayon will not look as bright as the rayon.

8. Weave structure is a factor when choosing colours. A weave that brings more of the warp or weft to the surface affects colour differently from one showing equal amounts of both. A porous fabric with a low number of ends and picks per centimetre gives an entirely different colour impression from one that is firmly and tightly constructed.

Detail of scarf (*left*) showing how yarn colours change when interwoven. The three swatches (*right*) are all woven on the same warp. The different combinations are the result of changing the weft colours and weave

YARNS

Yarns To weavers, yarns are the raw materials of their creations. They are both a source of inspiration and limitation.

Weaving is a craft of touching as well as seeing. The way a yarn feels between your fingers guides you to use it in the proper way or to explore in new directions for different uses. You should take the time to 'get to know' your yarns before you begin to weave.

One yarn can enhance another or detract from it. Textured yarns mixed together can create their own patternwork. All sorts of wonderful discoveries are possible and, when you add the heady element of colour, it is easy to understand why weavers say that there is never enough time to try all the experiments they have in mind. However, all is not done with wild abandon. There are a few ground rules that, if followed, can save a lot of frustration.

Warp yarns The first step in weaving is choosing the the yarn for the warp and weft. The warp will be under tension and must be ready to take much strain and wear as the weft is woven into it. Not all yarns can be used for the warp, although just about any yarns can be used for the weft – even reeds or long grasses picked in the fields.

Even though the warp *must* be strong to withstand the weaving process, it does not necessarily have to be made of heavy or thick yarns. Some synthetic yarns are almost gossamer fine, yet are extremely strong. The properties of the yarn to be used depend on how the woven article will be used.

If a yarn is not marked for warp use and you are unsure of its strength, test to see if it breaks or frays easily. A yarn that clings together is best avoided by beginners, as extra caution and experience are needed to get a clear and wide shed.

For rugs and tapestries it is advisable to have a warp yarn that is exceptionally strong since it will undergo tremendous beating in the process of being covered. Wrapping twine and heavy string are excellent for carpet warps.

Weft yarns Weft is also known as picks, filling or woof. Besides weaving yarns, you can use embroidery, knitting, crocheting and sewing yarns and threads. Do not hesitate to mix novelty yarns with plain yarns, dull with lustrous, soft furry with hard twist, and thick with very fine. The only restraint a beginner should exercise is in combining *too many* varieties of different textures or thickness in one fabric.

Some textured novelty yarns of various weights and strengths available to the handweaver

Weaving with materials other than yarn. Details of screen, woven of bark strips, wool, and square wooden beads, by Hella Skowronski. Photograph by Don Normark

Warp yarns stand out stronger than the weft yarns if the warp is dense in the reed (ie, if there are many ends per centimetre). The weft will be stronger if the number of warp ends per centimetre is less than the weft picks per centimetre. A pick or shot is a single thread of weft.

A new texture or colour can be achieved by twisting two dissimilar yarns or colours together in one pick.

The yarn should fit the purpose of the project. For

example, don't have scratchy or stiff yarns in dress fabrics, blankets or towels.

If you have doubts about how a yarn will look, weave a small trial or sample swatch. The lessons learned in making these swatches are invaluable.

FIBRES

Fibres Fibres twisted together make a yarn. Longer fibres produce stronger yarns than shorter fibres.

Two yarns of varying weights untwisted to show how many strands make up each ply

Linen, cotton, wool and silk are the most common natural fibres; of these, linen has the least elasticity, wool the most.

Synthetics usually have less elasticity than natural fibres. Common synthetics are rayon, nylon, orlon, zefran, and fibreglass, and of these, rayon is the most used and most available to the weaver. Synthetics are found alone or in combination with natural fibres or other synthetics. Each synthetic fibre has its own properties just as a natural fibre has.

When the fibres are spun, they are twisted together to form a continuous thread or yarn of a certain size and strength. The finished strand is given a number determined by the amount of yarn it takes to make up a pound. This number, called the *count*, designates the size or thickness of the yarn. A fine yarn has more lengths per pound, therefore it will carry a higher number than a heavy, coarse yarn. This is true of linen, cotton, wool and spun silk.

A denier system, based on weights per length, is used for filament silk and most synthetics. Here the reverse is true (ie, the coarser the yarn, the higher the number; the finer the yarn, the lower the number).

If a strand of yarn is used alone, it is called a singles. When two or more single threads are twisted together, they form a ply. This is designated by two numbers. For example, a number such as 20/2 means that the yarn is made of two strands of 20 singles. The smaller number indicates the amount of strands twisted together; the larger number indicates the thickness of a single strand. Most weaving yarns are 2, 3 or 4 ply. When you are buying yarn and find no indication of length per kilogram, the following table will help to determine the amount needed. The table is based on a certain number of lengths per pound of each fibre. The number varies from fibre to fibre.

Cotton	No 1 yarn	1 lb = 840 yds
Wool Galashiels cut	No 1 yarn	1 lb = 200 yds
Yorkshire skein	No 1 yarn	1 lb = 256 yds
Worsted Wool (plied)	No 1 yarn	1 lb = 560 yds
Linen	No 1 yarn	1 lb = 300 yds
Spun Silk	No 1 yarn	1 lb = 840 yds

Count systems based on metric units:

All yarns	Tex	Weight in grammes of one kilometre
Continuous filament yarns (man-made fibres and thrown silk)	Denier	Weight in grammes of nine kilometres
Spun yarns (cotton, wool, linen, spun silk, staple man-made fibres)	Metric	Number of kilometres to the kilogram

The Tex system can be used with the multiples and submultiples of kilotex and millitex for kilograms and milligrams per kilometre, respectively. (Tex is due to be the only system in use by 1975.)

To find the number of yards for a plied yarn, divide the ply number into the yarn number and multiply the result by the correct yardage above. For example, to find the yards per pound of 20/2 cotton:

$$20 \div 2 = 10 \times 840 = 8400 \text{ yds per lb}$$

To find the length per kilogram of a plied yarn in metric units, divide the length per kilogram of the base yarn by the ply number. For example, to find the length per kilogram of a 10/2 metric count yarn:

$$10 \text{ metric} = 10 \text{ km per kg}$$

$$10/2 \text{ metric} = \frac{10}{2} = 5 \text{ km per kg}$$

Museum pieces are sources of colour inspiration. This fragment (*above left*) of an ancient Peruvian textile provided the colour scheme for the poncho. (See page 84)

Black-eyed Susans (*above left*) suggested the colour scheme for the gold Greek bag (see page 66). A seashore scene (*below left*) suggested colour and design for the tapestry (*below right*). (See page 70)

Robert Dunne, Photo Researchers

To find the length per kilogram of a 100/2 tex yarn:

$$100 \text{ tex} = 100 \text{ gm/km}$$

$$\text{length of 1 kg of yarn} = \frac{1000}{100} = 10 \text{ km}$$

$$\text{length of 100/2 tex} = \frac{10}{2} \text{ km} = 5 \text{ km}$$

In many blends and novelty twists, it is difficult to determine the yards per pound, and if the supplier has not noted it on the label or price sheet, I would suggest writing to him for this information.

However, for spun silk, you have to multiply the ply and yarn numbers instead of dividing. For example, 20/2 spun silk would be calculated as follows:

$$20 \times 2 = 40, \ 40 \times 840 = 33{,}600 \text{ yds per lb}$$

COLOUR PLANNING

Nature, the greatest source of inspiration, offers limitless ideas for colour schemes and patterns. Some are to be found in the spontaneous groupings of wildflowers, the graining and marbling of rocks, or the white and cream tones of seashells that have been tempered by sand and sea.

Colour is not limited to field and shore; there is much in cities to inspire us in the ivy-covered bricks and weathered stones of buildings or in patterns of structural beams and the shadows they create.

Not to be overlooked are the collections of paintings and the relics of former cultures assembled in museums, and the exotically coloured marine and wildlife in aquariums and zoos.

As if there weren't enough in our natural surroundings to stimulate our search for ideas, we also have available beautifully coloured photographs in magazines. We should study these to see how colour groupings have been arranged and how designs have been balanced. Notice how the colours blend and observe the harmonious effect of one colour placed against another.

One observation that I feel we can all benefit by is noticing the proportions in nature, or in a painting or photograph. There is just the right balance between the spots on a butterfly's wing and the colour of the entire wing. The same is true of a painting we admire. There is just enough of each colour to make the whole composition unified. To get this unity is what we should all strive for, whether we are weaving a fabric, a cushion cover, a rug or a wall hanging.

If planning colours seems a bit mystifying at first, don't be discouraged; with just a little practice you will see how easy it is. And as you become increasingly aware of the colour that surrounds you, your heightened perceptions will enable you to create far more beautiful woven pieces.

The colours and design for the rya rug were adapted from a natural arrangement of waterlilies in a forest pond setting. There was no attempt in the colour sketch to duplicate the scene literally. Note the transition of this adaptation from simple colour impression to completed rug. The sketch is also a help to the weaver in selecting the proper yarn colours

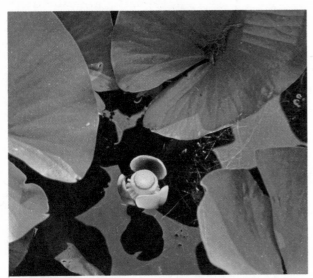

Irwin L. Oakes, Photo Researchers

DYEING OF YARNS

There will be times in the course of weaving when the colours available in yarn supply houses will not please you. Or, for some reason, the yarn you want cannot be found in the colour you need. This happens even though the handweaver today has a greater choice of yarns in a wider range of colours than ever before. There is no reason for you to become discouraged, however, or even to abandon that planned project. Just get ready for another adventure – dye your own yarn!

Dyeing yarn is a craft that could take several volumes to cover thoroughly. This book only hopes to skim the surface of its possibilities and to encourage you to try your hand at it. Lack of the right colour is only one reason for dyeing yarns. It is also the practical approach if you want to change the colour of leftover yarns or those yarns bought in wild or thoughtless moments. There are also effects and shadings you can get only by home dyeing.

It is not necessary to be surrounded by huge bubbling cauldrons in order to attain lovely results. In a small apartment kitchen the same delightful colours can come into being, and with a minimum of time and fuss. When I first decided to dye my own yarns, I set a special day apart and prepared for a long ordeal. I soon found it to be a stimulating interlude, one that I look forward to now as a period of relaxation after a hard day.

The principle of dyeing yarns can be simply outlined. The dye is mixed with hot water; into this the pre-soaked yarn is immersed and stirred. The dye fastens itself upon the yarn or interacts with it. Dyes are usually classified as natural or artificial and we will discuss both. Keep in mind that all yarns must be clean and the water used should be soft.

METHODS OF OBTAINING AND CHANGING COLOURS

Dyeing over unbleached or white yarn The easiest to handle since there is no colour in the yarn to affect the new one. You can get anything from a pastel to a deep shade, depending on how much dye is used. If you do not want the full intensity of colour, add either a touch of grey or the complement to the dye-bath.

Dyeing over grey or beige yarn A softer or greyer tone will be produced since the full intensity of the dye can not be attained.

Bleaching dyed yarn to get a lighter colour This can be done to some extent by soaking and washing dyed yarn in a detergent bath. To take out a little more colour, heat the bath to a simmering point. If you want the shade still lighter, a household bleach can be used, but follow label directions carefully, especially in regard to fibre content, since too much bleach will weaken some yarns. Always rinse thoroughly after bleaching. Do not become over-zealous in your efforts to lighten the colour for yarn appears darker when wet. Let it dry before judging its true shade. Test a small quantity of yarn first and keep a record of the proportion of bleach or detergent to water. Even bleaching, like even dyeing, calls for complete immersion of the yarn and occasional stirring while soaking.

Changing yarn colour by dyeing light or pastel hues a deeper tone Adding a colour of the same family will produce a deeper shade. For example, if you have a light pink but want a rose, dye over it with a deeper shade in its own colour family. If you use a complement, or a neighbouring colour on the colour wheel (see page 18), all manner of muted or brilliant tones can be achieved. But restrain yourself from putting in too much of the new colour. A gradual build-up will produce the desired result more often than trying to hit the shade right on the mark the first time. These experiments can be tried on solid colour yarns or on tweed mixtures.

Greying a bright colour Any strong colour can be greyed with a weak dye of its complement, or one of grey. Be sure that it is a *weak* dye-bath; too strong a solution will result in a mud colour.

Relating many different colours If you have yarn in colours that you feel do not relate, dye the whole batch in a common bath. They can be as widely separated on the colour wheel as red, yellow and blue – or of the same colour family as red, rust and orange. Choose a new colour, or a dye-bath of the complement, and the yarns will emerge from the bath with a colour harmony that unites them.

Ikat dyeing or **tie and dye** The technique known as Ikat dyeing comes to us from southeast Asia, where it was used to produce a variety of patterns. Sections of either the warp or weft can be dyed in this manner. Tie waxed cord evenly and tightly around the yarn so that no dye can penetrate to them. Tie at intervals according to the pattern desired.

Dip dyeing The objective here is to get varied shades in the yarn. For this process, dip one end of the yarn into the dye-bath while holding the rest of it out of the solution. Then dye another section and continue doing so until the yarn is all dyed. Use either one dye-bath of the same colour in intensities varying from strong to weak or several baths of different colours. If you use different colours, be careful not to overlap them or there will be muddy intervals in the yarn.

Piece dyeing This is a way to achieve unusual colour effects and shadings in the already woven cloth. Different fibres will absorb the dyes in varying degrees, and some not at all.

Dyeing a deeper shade or black If your previous attempts have produced very uneven colours, or ones that you cannot use, dye them a deeper shade or black. Dyeing black over some colours, especially red, may not produce a true deep black. In this case, add a little of the complement to the dye-bath. By over-dyeing black, past errors can be eliminated, and no yarn ever wasted. But beware of this 'crutch' or you will soon have a yarn bin full of home-dyed black yarn.

EQUIPMENT NEEDED

Soft water A few drops of acetic acid or vinegar will sometimes soften hard water.

Large enamel pan This will be used as the dye pot. I prefer a white one so that I can see the exact colour of the bath and not the reflected colour of the pan. The pan should be large enough to contain sufficient water to cover the yarn without crowding it. Stainless steel and copper can also be used.

Wooden or glass rods and spoon These are for lifting the yarn and stirring the bath. On one occasion I resorted to long, wooden chopsticks I had at home and found them very adequate. If you use the wooden rods, be sure to have a different one for every colour. Tongs, such as the ones used for Easter eggs dyeing, are also good for lifting yarn out of the bath.

Plastic or enamel buckets or pans For wetting-out or soaking the yarn and for rinsing after dyeing. Different pans will be needed unless you can successfully rotate both processes in the same container. You could also do both in the sink, but be sure to have a pan in which to carry the dripping yarn as you go from stove to sink.

Rubber gloves and an apron Dye will sometimes splatter so it is wise to wear a large cover-all apron or old clothes. The rubber gloves are necessary only if you mind having dye on your hands. Most dye will come off by scrubbing with Lava or Fels-Naptha soap, lemon juice, or weak solutions of bleaching agents.

A glass measuring cup For mixing a concentrate of the dye.

Soap flakes For the wetting-out process that takes place before the yarn is dyed. This helps the dye to penetrate further into the yarn.

Common salt This is used at the end to exhaust the dye-bath.

Glass jars with lids You should have some rather large ones in case you want to save the dye-bath and smaller ones in which to save the dye solution.

NOTE If, after you have finished dyeing your yarns, you find you have colours that you never expected to get and don't want to dye all of them black, put them aside and plan a later project around them. No yarn need ever be thrown out or wasted. You will be surprised at the weaving ideas some unexpected colour results will give you.

Be sure to keep accurate and complete records of the dye-baths. In a notebook, attach samples of yarns before and after dyeing and mark down beneath them the formula used for each shade. This will prove invaluable when you want to duplicate a shade later. If, however, in spite of your record keeping, nothing seems to approximate the colour you want when you try to match it on successive days, do not be upset. Part of the fascination of home dyeing is the subtle variations of colour obtained. Use this to advantage in your handweaving.

(*Above*) Ikat-dyed tapestry by Karen Chang, in the process of being woven. (*Right*) The completed tapestry

Common Dye-bath: yarns of different colours, but of same fibre content, before and after immersion in a common dye-bath. The original colours have caused variations in the dyed colours. **Dip-dye**: sections of the skein were dipped in different dye-baths producing variegated shades in one skein. Care was taken not to overlap the colours which would have produced muddy intervals in the yarn. **Diluted Dye-bath**: two yarns of the same fibre content. (*Right*) The yarn was dyed in a full-strength bath. (*Left*) The yarn was dyed in the same bath, diluted

COMMON DYE-BATH   DIP-DYE   DILUTED DYE-BATH

COMMERCIAL DYES

Commercial or artificial dyes can be bought in many shops, and there are also other brands that can be sent away for. They are all easy to handle, but the success of the project depends on following instructions carefully and in selecting the proper dye for a particular fibre. The packages usually contain an amount that will dye a whole pound of white yarn to full intensity of the colour indicated. General instructions follow for the use of commercial dyes.

1. Be sure the yarn is clean. Wind it into skeins and tie loosely but securely. If tied too tightly, rings will appear where the dye could not penetrate.

2. Prepare a wetting-out bath of warm water and a small amount of soap flakes. Soak the yarn in this bath for about ten minutes, or until saturated.

3. While the yarn is soaking, have the water for the dye-bath simmering on the stove. There should be enough water in the bath to completely cover the yarn. Put the dye in the measuring cup and dissolve with hot water. This can be a paste mixture or a watery solution, depending on the dye used. Follow package directions carefully.

4. Pour some of the dye concentrate into the bath,

A dye-bath on yarns of same colours but of different fibre content

A dye-bath on yarns of different colours but same fibre content

Piece dyeing is done to change or to correct the colour of a woven fabric. Place mat is shown before and after dyeing but in small amounts. If the yarn dries too light, you can always redye it with a stronger solution; if you add too much dye, and the yarn dries too deep, you will have the harder job of removing some of the colour.

5. Take the yarn out of the wetting-out bath and squeeze dry.

6. Put the yarn into the dye-bath. Stir so that there will be even penetration. Keep at a simmering point until you have the shade you are after, or until the dye-bath is exhausted. Remember that wet yarn will appear darker than dry yarn. Read the timing instructions that come with your particular dye.

7. Add the hot water that has been simmering on the stove to the dye-bath for the next skein or colour change. From one dye-bath, you can get several others. Just add hot water to replace any taken up by the preceding batches, and more dyestuff, if necessary, of the same colour or a new colour.

8. When using artificial dyes, it is a good idea to add a tablespoon of common salt to the dye-bath at the end of the dyeing period. This will exhaust whatever dye is left.

9. When the yarn is the colour you want, lift it from the dye-bath and transfer it to the rinsing bath. Allow most of the dye to drip back into the pot.

10. Rinse the yarn in a bath only slightly cooler than the dye-bath, then progress to successively cooler baths until the water runs clear. The last bath can be quite cool.

11. After the final rinsing, squeeze the yarn – do not wring – and hang in a shaded place to dry.

12. Save any leftover dye by putting it in the large covered containers. The concentrate will go into the small containers. Be sure that all are accurately labelled.

13. During this entire process, you should be noting down amounts of dyestuff, water, etc.

NATURAL DYES

The directions listed thus far apply for the most part to artificial dyes, but there is another category of dyes obtained from natural substances such as roots, lichens, buds, leaves, flowers, berries, seeds, twigs, branches and tree bark. The dyes from nature can be used alone or in combination with each other.

Part of the attraction of dyeing with natural substances are the excursions to the woods and fields that are made in order to gather the dyestuffs. However, if you are unable to do this, there are household items that also produce natural dyes. Among these are onion skins, coffee, tea and cinnamon bark.

Many natural dyes change colour according to the mordant used. A mordant is a substance that binds the colour to the fibre through a chemical action with the dye. Mordanting controls the colours of dyes and makes them permanent. It can be done before, during or after dyeing.

There is a little bit more uncertainty with natural dyes than with artificial ones. You should not expect to find it easy to repeat the same colour at another dyeing, and it is also a game of chance to arrive at the exact colour you want in the first place. Besides the variables encountered in the kitchen when we prepare the dyestuff, we must take into account that the natural sources of the dye may differ according to region and season. The soil it grows in, the length of the summer's warmth, the amount of sun and rainfall are all factors that produce differences. But don't be put off trying natural dyes. Yarns dyed in this manner have a warmth and softness of colour never achieved in a commercial dye house. Their loveliness more than compensates for any difficulties you may encounter when dealing with them.

Following is a very general set of directions on how to obtain and use the natural dyestuff:

1. Gather the dyestuff. Clean of foreign matter, dry and crush, unless it is to be used fresh. Since many natural dyestuffs are seasonal, it is best to gather them when you can, then dry and store them.

2. Put a small amount of water into an enamel bowl and steep the dyestuff from two hours to overnight.

3. After steeping, boil for half an hour to two hours.

4. Strain off liquid through cheesecloth. Save the remaining solid matter by wrapping it in several layers of cheesecloth. This can be covered with water and reboiled for about an hour.

5. Add 18 litres (4 gallons) of water to the dyestuff. Heat to lukewarm.

6. Add the wetted-out wool. If the mordant has already been added to the wool, the last rinsing out of the mordant should have been in water of the same temperature as the dye-bath. If the mordanting is to follow dyeing, then the yarn should be rinsed out in a lukewarm bath.

7. Bring the dye-bath to a simmer and continue simmering for the time indicated in your recipe.

8. Remove the yarn from the bath when dyeing is complete. Rinse first in a hot bath, then progress to successively cooler baths until the water runs clear.

9. Dry in the shade after squeezing out excess water.

MORDANTS

Before Dyeing Yarns

Wool should be thoroughly washed of its grease in a mild soap flake bath. If it should dry between this bath and mordanting, be sure to wet it out again. The mordant bath is a solution of 115 gm (4 oz) of alum (less for lighter shades) and 28·5 gm (1 oz) of cream of tartar to 18 to 20 litres (4-4½ gals) of water. Use soft water at a warm temperature. Dissolve alum and cream of tartar first in a small amount of water, then add it to the warm water. Add the wool to the warm mordant and bring slowly to a simmer. Keep at a simmer for an hour, stirring occasionally with a glass rod. Remove from mordant, rinse thoroughly, and take to the dye-bath or dry.

Silk is mordanted the same as wool, but both *raw silk* and *spun silk* contain a waxy gum that must be removed. For raw silk, boil off the gum in a strong soap bath; for spun silk, wash it off in a warm soap bath.

Cotton, Linen and Rayon Are Mordanted in Three Solutions

The first solution contains 115 (4 oz) of alum and 28·5 gm (1 oz) of washing soda to 18 litres (4 gals) of water. Boil one hour and keep overnight in the mordant.

Squeeze out and put in a bath of 28·5 gm (1 oz) tannic acid to 20 litres (4½ gals) of water. Keep at a slight simmer for one hour. Cool and let stand overnight.

Remove and rinse slightly, then repeat step No 1. Rinse the yarn the next day, squeeze out excess water, and put it into the dye-bath.

After Dyeing Yarns

After removing the yarn from the dye-bath, put it into a 5% solution of tannic acid to 4·5 litres (1 gal) of water. Let it stay for thirty minutes, then remove to a new solution of 5% tartar emetic and 4·5 litres (1 gal) of water for fifteen minutes. Rinse thoroughly and dry.

USE CAUTION WITH THE TARTAR EMETIC SINCE IT IS A POISON.

If only part of the skein is put into the mordant, it will be a different colour than the rest of the skein. If you are adding a mordant to a dye-bath to deepen a colour, do so sparingly – use small pinches of the mordant.

There are other mordants that can be used, such as chrome, iron sulphate and slaked lime. The type of mordant and amount used depend on the colour you are after. I have been fortunate in finding mordant supplies at my corner drugstore and supermarket. If you live in a locality where such things are not easily come by, ask your druggist to order small amounts for you.

It is well to approach natural dyeing with a feeling of experimentation. You will then be surprised and delighted with the colour that results – whether or not it is the one you want.

On page 31 is a list of common plants and trees from which we can obtain many lovely shades. The rule-of-thumb ratio that I have used in the formulae for natural dyeing has been ·454 kg (1 lb) of dry wool to ·454 kg (1 lb) of the dyestuff to 18 to 20 litres (4 to 4½ gals) of water. If you wish to dye ·225 kg (½ lb), or even ·115 kg (¼ lb), then, of course, halve or quarter the amounts of water and dry substance. More than ·454-kg (1-lb) lots of wool might be difficult to handle. Put in more of the dyestuff if the colour comes out too weak.

As you can see, the world of dyeing – whether with artificial or natural dyes – offers unlimited fields for exploration and experimentation. We have just scratched the surface. *Do* go on and see what lies beneath it – but with this caution: don't get so intrigued by dyeing yarns that you forget your weaving.

NATURAL DYE SOURCES

Various natural dye sources and the colours obtained from them. The colour on the left is full strength and the tint on the right is half strength

WHITE BIRCH LEAF

WHITE BIRCH TWIG

BLUEBERRY

DANDELION

LILY OF THE VALLEY

MARIGOLD

ONION SKINS

SUMAC

DYESTUFF	SOURCE	COLOUR	MORDANT	MISCELLANEOUS NOTES
ALDER	BARK, LEAVES BARK	BLACK BROWN	IRON SULPHATE	
AZALEA	LEAVES LEAVES	DARK GREY BROWNISH RED	WEAK IRON SULPHATE SLAKED LIME	PICK LEAVES IN LATE FALL
BAYBERRY	LEAVES	GREYISH GREEN	ALUM	PICK LEAVES IN SUMMER
BLACKBERRY	YOUNG SHOOTS	LIGHT GREY TO BLACK	ALUM	ADD IRON SULPHATE TO DEEPEN COLOUR
BLACK WALNUT	GREEN OUTER HUSKS	DARK BROWN TO BLACK	NO MORDANT NEEDED, BUT SOAK SHELLS WELL	PICK HUSKS WHILE GREEN, REMOVE BY POUNDING WITH HAMMER*
BLUEBERRY	BERRY	BLUE TO PURPLE	ALUM	
DANDELION	ROOTS WHOLE PLANT	PURPLE MAGENTA	NO MORDANT NEEDED	
ELDERBERRY	BERRY BERRY BERRY LEAVES	BLUE LILAC VIOLET TO PURPLE GREEN	SALT ALUM CHROME ALUM	CRUSH BERRIES BEFORE SOAKING DEPTH OF COLOUR DEPENDS ON AMOUNT USED AND LENGTH OF BOILING
GOLDENROD	FLOWER	YELLOW-TAN OLD GOLD	ALUM CHROME	PICK WHEN FLOWERS ARE JUST ABOUT TO BLOOM
LILY OF THE VALLEY	LEAVES	LIME GREENY GOLD	CHROME CHROME	PICK IN SPRING PICK IN FALL
MARIGOLD	FLOWER	YELLOW TO GOLD	ALUM	ADD A FEW WALNUT HUSKS FOR A DEEPER TONE
MAPLE	BARK BARK	GREY TO PURPLE OLIVE	IRON SULPHATE ALUM	
NETTLE	WHOLE PLANT	GREENISH YELLOW	ALUM	WEAR GLOVES WHEN PICKING OR AN ITCHY RASH WILL DEVELOP
ONION	DRIED SKINS FROM COMMON COOKING ONION	GOLDEN-YELLOW BURNT ORANGE BRASS YELLOW OLIVE GREEN	ALUM ALUM WITH TIN CHROME ALUM WITH IRON SULPHATE	MORDANT WOOL FIRST WITH ALUM
POMEGRANATE	HARD OUTER SKIN	YELLOW BROWN VIOLET BLUE	ALUM VERY WEAK IRON SULPHATE SOLUTION ABOVE SOLUTION PLUS ASH EXTRACT	
PRIVET	BERRIES BERRIES AND LEAVES LEAVES AND BRANCH TIPS	BLUE, BLUE GREEN GREEN YELLOW GOLD	ALUM AND SALT ALUM ALUM AND CREAM OF TARTAR CHROME	ADD YARN WHEN CRUSHED BERRIES ARE BOILING
SAFFRON	FLOWERS OR POWDER FROM GROCERY	YELLOW	ALUM	
SUMAC	BERRIES LEAVES, TWIGS	YELLOWISH TAN TO GREY BROWN TO BLACK	ALUM AND IRON SULPHATE NO MORDANT NEEDED	PICK WHEN FULLY RIPE, CRUSH FRUIT BEFORE OVERNIGHT SOAKING, ADD IRON SULPHATE AFTER DYE
WHITE BIRCH	LEAVES TWIGS INNER BARK	YELLOW YELLOWISH GREEN BROWN	ALUM ALUM NO MORDANT NEEDED	LONGER BOILING WILL PRODUCE A DEEPER YELLOW BREAK BARK INTO SMALL BITS BEFORE SOAKING

*USE RUBBER GLOVES, AS DYE WILL STAIN. FOR DARK BROWNS, ADD IRON SULPHATE.
FOR BLACK, ADD ALSO A HANDFUL OF SUMAC BERRIES. LEAVE OVERNIGHT IN DYE-BATH.

WARPING

Warping is part of the process known as dressing the loom, the object being to get the calculated number of warp ends in the right arrangement and of the same length and tension. Warp ends is the term used when referring to the individual lengths or pieces of warp.

Warping is a prelude to weaving. A well-made warp will make the hours spent at the actual weaving that much more enjoyable. At first, warping will require patience from you. But, after enough warps have been put on, your gestures in warp-making will become instinctive and rhythmic, and you will find this as relaxing and enjoyable as weaving itself.

TO PREPARE YARN FOR WARPING

When making the warp by any of the methods for floor and table looms, it is necessary to have the yarn in skeins, cones or spools. These have to be on a fixture that allows the yarn to revolve off smoothly as it is needed for the warp. Spools are usually put on spool racks, cones on yarn holders, and skeins on swifts. If these are not available, you can make substitutes. A yarn holder that will hold spools or cones can be made by hammering nails, about 10 to 12·75 cm (4 to 5 in) long, through a piece of sturdy wood. The nails should be spaced about 15·25 cm (6 in) apart. Spools or balls of yarn can be put into boxes with high sides so that they will not tumble out as the yarn is revolved off.

CONE

SKEIN

SPOOL

UNWOUND SKEIN

Yarns are packaged for sale in several ways, the most common of which are shown above

Skeins can be placed around chairs. However, this method does not allow for the rapid flow of yarn.

CALCULATIONS

To arrive at the number of warp ends needed, you must decide how wide you want your woven piece to be, and how heavy or dense. The density of a fabric is determined by the number of warp ends per centimetre, or sett. A good formula to follow is:

sett × width in cm = total number of ends

For example:

sett of 4 ends per cm × width of 25 cm = 4 × 25 =
100 warp ends
(10 ends/in. × 10 in. = 10 × 10 = 100 ends)

To the total number of ends should be added an additional amount to compensate for the pulling in at the selvedges of the warp by the weft. A general rule of thumb is to add 10% of the finished width. The total number of ends in the above example is now 110. Professionally, this is calculated according to fibre content and resiliency of the yarn.

The second calculation is to determine the length of the warp ends that will be put on the loom so that your finished fabric will be the length you want. The formula for this is:

finished length
+ loom allowance
+ take up
= dressed length

Loom allowance is the amount wasted in putting the warp on the loom; also, it is the amount remaining on the loom, in and behind the shafts, that cannot be woven off. For a floor loom allow 1 to 1·5 metres, and for a table loom 0·5 m.

The warp is under tension while it is being woven, but this tension is released as soon as the fabric is taken from the loom. In order to compensate for the difference between the tense and the released states, we must add the take up.

The take up is literally the yarn taken up in the inter-weaving process as the weft goes over and under the warp. Various fibres have various take ups, such as:

wool 16·5 cm per m	6 in. per yd
linen 8·5 cm per m	3 in. per yd
mixed yarn 11–14 cm per m	4 to 5 in. per yd

An example of the above formula follows – the problem being how much warp is needed if a 5-m piece of wool and silk is to be woven. It will be woven on a floor loom.

finished length	5 m (5½ yds)
+ loom allowance	1 m (1 yd 4 in.)
+ take up of 14 cm per m	0·70 m (¾ yd)
= dressed length	6·70 m (7¼ yds, approx)

The calculations for the total number of ends apply to all looms, but the calculations for the length apply only to floor and table looms. When working on the frame loom, you are limited to a warp twice the length of the loom.

WARPING METHOD No 1 – USING A WARPING REEL

A warping reel or drum is one method used to prepare the warp for a floor or table loom. In the most common of reels, there is 0·5 m (20 in.) between each side dowel. A complete trip around the reel would then be 2 m (6 ft 8 in.).

Always hold the yarn taut while warping and maintain even tension throughout the whole warping operation.

Start the warp at the bottom of the reel by tying the yarn to the peg on the bottom horizontal bar. There is also a horizontal bar at the top around whose pegs the *cross* is formed. These bars may be shifted from one side of the reel to another in order to get the desired length of warp.

Warping method No 1: preparing the warp on a warping reel, or drum. Here the yarn is fed from a cone on a holder, onto the warping reel. Note the two crosses, one at the top and one at the bottom. Only one cross is necessary, but two are recommended for the beginner in the event that one cross is lost

To make the warp (with crosses at both top and bottom horizontal bars), secure the beginning end at E with a loop knot around the peg. Go under D and up and around as many times as necessary for the desired length. Go under C and over B and A. You have now made one warp end, but *do not* cut the end. Continue by going under A and B and over C, return down and around to D, then over D and back under E. You are now beginning the third warp end. Proceed in this manner until the total number of warp ends is reached. If it is an even number, tie and cut off at E. If it is an odd number, tie and cut off at A.

Close-up of cross tied before it is chained off the reel

The cross that is formed on the upper horizontal bar is also called a lease. Its function is to keep the warp ends in order until the warp is completely threaded through the loom. It is possible to make a second cross on the bottom horizontal bar. This is advisable for beginners so that if one cross is lost, there will be the other one to keep the threads from tangling.

Before you take the warp off the reel, tie the cross in a contrasting colour yarn so that it will not be lost in its transference to the loom. Also, at every metre, tie the contrasting yarn around the entire group of warp threads. This is called a choke and keeps the yarns from tangling while the chain is being made and while the warp is being prepared on the loom.

CHAINING

In order to conveniently carry the warp from the reel to the loom, the length of the warp is reduced by chaining it. The chain is similar to a crochet chain, and the hand is used like a crochet hook in making it. For those unfamiliar with crocheting, the following illustrations explain the technique.

Flip the end of the warp over the hand so that it forms a loop. Pull the warp through the loop until it forms another loop. Through this loop repeat the same procedure – and so on, until the whole warp is chained

STEP 1

STEP 3

STEP 2

STEP 4

The chained warp ready to be taken to the loom from the warping reel

off. Do not pull the last loop completely through, or you will lock the chain so that it cannot be unchained later on the loom.

WARPING METHOD No 2 – USING A WARPING BOARD

This is an alternate method of warping for the floor or table loom. The board can be placed on a table or hung from a wall. A common size for the warping board is 0·5 m by 1 m (20 in. × 3 ft 3½ in.).

After the warp has been determined, measure it off on the board. For example, a 3·5-m (4-yd) warp could start at A, go *over* the peg at B, around at C and over to D, back and around at D to E, around the side at E, up to F, over F and G and under and over H. This is the route of one 3·5-m (4-yd) warp end. The warp is continued by returning under G, over F down to E across to D, back across the board to C, across and under B, and up and around A. This is now the beginning of the third warp end.

Continue for the needed number. Then tie the crosses and the chokes, chain and remove to the loom as explained in warping method No 1.

NOTE If you should find it difficult to keep count of the warp ends, mark off every group of 20 with a loose loop of contrasting yarn.

Alternate Methods of Warping

If you have no warping reel or board, methods can be improvised that will do the job just as well. The important points to remember are always to maintain even tension and to have a cross.

1. Three pegs driven into the ground out-of-doors. Peg A and peg C are placed as far apart as the length of the desired warp. The cross is formed between pegs A and B.

2. Kitchen chairs. These must be weighted down so that they will not shift during the warping operation. Avoid those with ornamental knobs, otherwise you will find it difficult to pull off the warp when you are through. The cross can be formed between the chairs, or made around broom handles or dowel rods at the sides of chairs.

3. Tables turned upside down or bedposts can also be used.

Warping method No 2: preparing the warp on a warping board

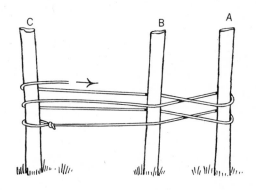

Alternate methods of warping. (*Above*) Three pegs driven into the ground. (*Below*) Weighted chairs used as a warping device

BEAMING AND THREADING THE LOOM

After the chained warp has been taken to the loom, it must be rolled (beamed) onto the warp beam, threaded (drawn-in) through the heddles, and threaded (sleyed) through the reed. One way of doing this is the back-to-front method. This means we will roll the warp onto the warp beam and thread from the back of the loom to the front.

1. Attach the warp to the warp beam by slipping the back apron bar through the loop formed by the warp near the cross.

2. Insert the lease rods into the warp on either side of the cross. One rod goes to the back of where the threads cross and the other rod goes in front. Lease rods are usually included with the purchase of a loom. If they are not included with your loom, you can use any smooth, flat, thin rods the correct width of the loom.

3. Tie the lease rods together and then to a cord running from the castle to the slabstock. They will maintain the cross while the warp is being beamed and may be removed when the sleying is finished.

4. Cut the contrasting yarn that holds the cross and spread the warp evenly to the width it is to be woven. A raddle or spreader may be used.

5. Maintain the warp under tension while it is being wound onto the warp beam. It would be best for a beginner to have a friend help so that while one holds the tension and combs the warp, the other can wind the warp beam. However, if this is not possible, then hold the warp over the castle as you wind, or bring the warp over the breast beam and attach weights to maintain the tension.

6. Stop every foot or more to shake out the warp gently and comb it with your fingers. This is done to prevent the ends from tangling and to catch any ends that may have slipped from tension.

7. Heavy paper or smooth sticks should be inserted between layers of the warp ends while beaming so that the warp will always have a smooth surface on which to maintain its tension.

8. The beaming is finished when there is only 30 cm (11¾ in.) of warp left in front of the first shaft. Cut the loop at this end of the warp and begin the drawing-in.

9. If the beater can be disassembled, do so, for then

LEASE RODS INSERTED INTO CROSS

WARP ATTACHED TO BACK APRON BAR

APRON

SHAFT FRAME

LEASE RODS

SLABSTOCK OR BACK BEAM

WARP END DRAWN THROUGH HEDDLE EYE

CASTLE

WARP BEAM

WARP BEING ROLLED AROUND WARP BEAM WHILE INSERTING PAPER

there will be no obstruction between you and the heddles while you are threading them.

10. Place the heddles you will be using in the centre of each shaft. Tie off the remaining heddles on each side.

11. With a reed hook, pull the warp end through the heddle eye, from back to front. Take the yarn in consecutive order from right to left, from the lease rod nearest to the back shaft. One end will come from *over* the lease rod and the other from *under*.

12. The warp ends are drawn in according to a warp plan, or drawing-in draft (see chapter on Drafting), which tells the shaft number of the heddle to be threaded. The shaft facing the weaver is shaft No 1 and the one facing the back beam is shaft No 4 (in a 4-shaft loom).

13. Check every 20 to 30 ends to see that the drawing-in is correct. Then tie the ends in a slipknot so that they will not pull out accidentally.

14. Find the centre of the reed and measure the width of your warp so that it is evenly spaced on each side of the centre mark.

15. Sley the warp ends through the dents in the reed according to the number that must go in each dent.

The projects to follow will indicate the number of ends per dent. Sley from right to left with the reed either in the beater or lying flat and supported by rods on the side. If in the former position, sley from back to front. If in the latter positions, sley from the top down. Be sure to take the warp ends in order so that they do not cross and thus prevent a clear shed from forming. Check and tie slipknots.

16. Tie a bundle, or grouping, of warp ends to the front apron bar. This should be about the thickness of a forefinger. First tie a group to the centre of the apron bar, then tie successive groups to the right and left of the centre. All the groups should be tied with a single knot, as shown in the diagram. Go over the groups from right to left and pull up on the knotted ends to adjust the tension. Pass your hand lightly over the warp at the back of the loom and, if you feel any loosening of tension, pull up on these warp ends in the groups. Adjust the tension in the knots a third time and double knot the groups to ensure that the ends do not slip out while being woven.

SHAFT FRAME

SLEYING ENDS THROUGH REED

SLIP KNOT-HOLDING ENDS IN FRONT OF REED

WARP END DRAWN THROUGH HEDDLE EYE

WARP TIED IN A BUNDLE TO FRONT APRON BAR

REED

FRONT APRON BAR

BREAST BEAM

SLIP KNOT IN FRONT OF HEDDLES

CLOTH BEAM WITH APRON

WARPING THE FRAME LOOM

The warp is made directly on the frame loom. No warping reel or board is required, nor is a cross, since the ends are put in position for weaving as the warp is being wound onto the loom. In this frame loom the warp is twice the length of the loom and can be revolved around it as the weaving progresses.

Even warp tension should always be maintained, but the ends do *not* need to be overly tight. If you find tension slackening as you are winding the warp around the loom, tug on the yarn until you find that all feels even again.

WARPING INSTRUCTIONS

1. Temporarily tape or tie the warp-end bar on the back of the loom. This is a precautionary measure to keep the bar from shifting at the beginning of warping.
2. With tape or pencil indicate the sett marks where you want the warp to begin and end. The warp ends must be spaced, while winding the warp, between every 1 cm sett mark at the required number of ends per cm. For example, if you are using a sett of 4 ends per cm (10 ends per inch), one warp end goes in the notch and 3 between each notch. Selvedge ends are counted two as one.
3. Before warping begins, tension sticks should be taped to the front of the loom at top and bottom. They are removed as the weaving progresses and the take-up tightens the warp.
4. Wind the warp yarn into a large bobbin; it can then be held in your hand, greatly facilitating going around the warp-end bar.
5. Unscrew the heddle rod while warping.
6. Tie the warp yarn around the warp-end bar at a point directly over the beginning sett mark.
7. Take the yarn down and around to the front of the loom, up to the top and over, down to the warp-end bar, around it and *back* to the top of the loom. Go down the front, under the bottom frame, up to the warp-end bar, around it and *back* to the bottom. Continue in this manner until the required number of ends have been warped.
8. After bringing the yarn around the warp-end bar,

BACK OF LOOM

START →   WARP-END BAR

The frame loom is warped from the back. After going around the warp-end bar, the warp always returns in the direction from which it came

return it in the direction from which it came in order for the warp to revolve around the loom. The yarns around the warp-end bar should look like the above drawing.
9. Tie the last end to the warp-end bar and cut it free of the bobbin. Remove tape holding the warp-end bar in place. Rescrew the heddle rod.

ARRANGEMENT FOR TWO SHEDS

The warp is complete; now we must make an arrangement that will give us the two sheds.

First shed The shed stick is used to make the first shed. Insert it at the right, above the heddle rod, and weave it *under* the *odd*-numbered ends and *over* the *even*-numbered ones. When all the ends are either over or under the shed stick, turn the stick on its edge at a right angle to the warp and check if your first shed is correct. Remember that the selvedge ends are counted two as one.
Second shed Heddles are made for the second shed. You will need strong linen cord, preferably in a natural colour, and a blunt-edged tapestry needle.

Close-up of heddle bar with string heddles attached through loops of heddle spacer

Chain spacer, the length of thread that is chained around and between the warp ends to separate them

1. Take a piece of linen cord 2 m (6 ft 7 in.) long and tie one end to the heddle rod on the right side of the loom, around the screw. Move 1·25 cm ($\frac{1}{2}$ in.) to the left and go over the rod with the cord, meanwhile holding a portion of the cord at the bottom of the rod. This forms a loop through which the cord goes after it circles the rod. This is called a half-hitch and is repeated over the entire rod at approximately 3-mm ($\frac{1}{8}$-in.) intervals. At the other end, tie the cord around the left screw.

2. Cut as many 25-cm ($9\frac{7}{8}$-in.) pieces of linen cord as there are even-numbered warp ends. These 25-cm pieces will become your actual heddles. Insert a piece of white paper between the back and front of the warp to aid you in seeing and picking up the warp ends.

3. Slip the 25-cm pieces of linen *under* the *even-numbered* warp ends. Using the needle, insert the linen thread into the loop of the heddle cord that is directly above the warp end you are working with. Double-knot the ends of the linen cord and the heddle is complete.

It is not necessary to put on completely new heddles for your next warp. The heddles are still usable if they are long enough to give a good shed when pulled on. All that is needed is to cut the knot, loop under the new warp end, and retie. When the heddles become too short to manipulate, cut off and put new ones on. The heddle cord at all times stays in place on the heddle rod.

THE CHAIN SPACER

The last thing to be done before we start weaving is to make a chain spacer at the bottom of the warp where the weaving will begin. This serves the triple function of spacing the warp evenly, keeping the ends

in order, and giving a firm starting edge for the first row of weft.

Steps to Follow:

1. The chain spacer should be placed so that there is enough unwoven warp between it and the warp-end bar to allow for a fringe, braid or any other method of finishing off. If the warp-end bar is so far up on the back of the loom as to cause too much unwoven warp to remain at the beginning of the piece, push the bar down towards the bottom.

2. Cut 1 m (3 ft 3$\frac{1}{2}$in.) of the same linen cord that was used for the heddles.

3. Tie it around the right side of the frame as shown.

4. Draw the long end of the cord from under the top warp, then pull enough of it up between the first and second ends to form a small loop. The chain is really a series of loops as in crochet and some weavers even use a crochet hook in making it.

5. With thumb and forefinger, go through this loop to the right and form another loop to the right of the first end. Always pull tightly on the new loop in the right hand so that all of the slack in the chain is drawn out and the finished loops are tightly and evenly spaced.

6. Pick up yet another loop between the second and third ends and pull through the held loop. Tighten.

7. Through this loop, pull the one formed between the third and fourth ends. This is continued until all the warp ends are enclosed in loops.

8. Pull the cord through the last loop, on the left side of the warp; this will lock the chain.

9. Tie the cord to the left side of the frame. Adjust the tie on the right side of the frame so that the warp is pulled out slightly wider than the intended width.

PREPARING THE WEFT

Once the loom is ready, we have only to prepare the weft before weaving can begin.

In order to do this, the yarn must be unwound from whatever holds it – spool, cone or skein – and, in small amounts, put on shuttles. These are implements designed to carry the weft through the open shed from one side of the loom to the other. Shuttles come in various forms, and the one you use will depend on the width of the shed opening and the weight of the yarn.

USING THE STICK SHUTTLE

The stick shuttle is long and flat and can be easily made at home out of wood or heavy cardboard. It varies in length from 23 cm (9 in.) to 56 cm (22 in.). This shuttle carries heavy weft yarns or rags and is used on looms that give only narrow shed openings.

STICK SHUTTLE

WEFT YARN BEING WOUND AROUND SHUTTLE

SHUTTLE READY FOR WEAVING

To put the yarn on the stick shuttle, loop one end of the yarn around an arm of the shuttle and then wind a substantial amount around its length. The end result should resemble the drawing above. Do not wind on too much yarn or else it will be difficult to get the shuttle through the shed. Also, broken warp ends may result if the weft yarn brushes either the top or bottom of the shed as the shuttle continually passes back and forth.

USING THE BOAT SHUTTLE

The boat shuttle is also made of wood, but it is used for lighter-weight weft yarns and on looms giving larger sheds. Since this shuttle is made so that it can be thrown from one side of the shed to the other, it is what we use when weaving wide fabrics. Boat shuttles come in a variety of types and sizes. Some come equipped with rollers on the bottom which make them glide through the shed even faster.

The boat shuttle has a steel pin in its centre section which holds a removable bobbin or quill. The weft yarn is wound around the bobbin, which is then slipped onto the pin with the starting end of the weft yarn threaded through the hole on one side of the shuttle. This hole always faces the weaver as the shuttle travels through the shed.

Most shuttles come with at least one bobbin, usually of plastic or cardboard. Extra ones can be made by rolling an oval-cut piece of heavy paper to the diameter and length of the bobbin needed. The paper must be sturdy or the bobbin will buckle in the centre.

(A) Boat shuttle with empty bobbin. (B) A paper quill can be used as an extra bobbin. (C) To make a quill, roll an oval piece of heavy paper and cut to the width and length needed. (D) Proper way of winding weft yarn around quill. (E) Boat shuttle with quill completely wound

WINDING THE BOBBIN FOR THE BOAT SHUTTLE

The weft yarn is wound by hand onto the bobbin or by electric or hand bobbin winders. Many clever weavers have made bobbin winders at home by inserting a steel rod into a small electric motor (such as in a portable mixer, sewing machine or drill).

In order to have the yarn wound on correctly, the two ends of the bobbin are built up first and the centre last. If the reverse were done, the yarn could not flow off easily during weaving. It is important to have bobbins tightly wound, for if they are not, the yarn will roll off at the ends and become entangled around the shuttle pin.

Winding the weft yarn from cone to bobbin on a hand bobbin winder

OTHER SHUTTLES

For weaving on upright looms or on frame looms, the weft carrier should be small so that when it hangs from the weaving it will not pull at the weft. A Gobelin bobbin (its point is used to beat down the weft) and Aubusson flute are of this type. A very small cardboard shuttle or a knitting bobbin are also practical. The use of the latter would be limited to an occasional colour since it holds only a small amount of yarn. The cardboard shuttle must have a slot on its edge in which to insert the yarn so that it won't unwind when the shuttle hangs idle by the side of the loom.

MAKING THE BUTTERFLY

On the frame loom, a butterfly of yarn can be used instead of a shuttle. A butterfly is an arrangement, or bundle, of weft yarn without a holder and is made by winding the yarn around the fingers in a figure of 8. Butterflies are most often used in making the pile on rugs. They are flexible and can easily go over and under warp ends and around a gauge which is used for making the rug pile knot.

Butterflies are made on the palm of the hand. The starting end of the yarn, as it comes from the skein or spool, is clasped between two fingers. The yarn is then brought behind and around the thumb and around the little finger from back to front. On its return trip to the thumb, the yarn should cross in the centre; this will keep it in order and free from tangles. When a suitable amount is thus wound, cut the yarn at its source and wind this loose end around the centre of the butterfly, half-hitching it twice so that it will not become undone. The other loose end, which is being held by the little finger, is the pulling end which releases the yarn for use.

NOTE Whether you are making butterflies or bobbins, do not be misled into thinking that if you make extra large ones, you will have to make less of them and thereby save yourself time. Outsize butterflies or bobbins are difficult to manipulate. They get caught in the warp, which could lead to broken ends, or they get knotted and tangled within themselves. This only results in a frayed temper and a loss of time.

(1) Making a butterfly by winding the yarn around the fingers in a figure of eight. **(2)** The completed butterfly

DRAFTING WEAVES

Weaves are the patterns we achieve in the cloth through an interaction between the way the warp is threaded through the heddles and the order in which the shafts are raised or lowered. In order for weavers to explain concisely and quickly what the weave will look like, how to thread the loom for a particular weave and what levers or treadles to press, they use a shorthand language called drafting.

For you to understand weaving fully and get the most enjoyment and fulfilment from it, you should try to read a draft, write one and ultimately design one.

UNDERSTANDING DRAFTING

In order to learn this shorthand language, you will need paper that is marked off into a number of small squares per cm. Called graph paper, it comes in various sizes. I have found either the 3-mm ($\frac{1}{8}$-in.) size or the 2·5-mm ($\frac{1}{10}$-in.) (ie, 8 or 10 squares to the inch respectively) to be the easiest on the eyes. You can also make your own graph paper by simply drawing lines that cross at right angles.

Whatever the size of the paper, it is important to keep in mind that a number of blocks on paper will equal the same number of warp ends even though they may not both equal a centimetre.

In most cases, the graph paper weave will be larger than the actual woven weave, and it is up to the weaver to make the mental adjustment between the paper and the cloth. This ability – to visualize the weave on paper, to plan it and to avoid mistakes in the pattern – is important to strive for while learning drafting.

Three ways to write a drawing-in draft, or warp plan. **(A)** Squares filled in. **(B)** Squares X'd in. **(C)** Squares numbered

When I first learned to draft in school, I naively believed there was only one way to write a draft. I have learned since that there are almost as many ways as there are weavers. However, the three methods illustrated (A, B, and C), are the ones generally used in weaving books and manuals.

TYPES OF DRAFTS

There Are Three Kinds of Drafts

Weave draft Indicates the pattern of the weave.
Warp plan Indicates how the loom should be threaded. Also called drawing-in draft or threading draft.
Lifting plan Indicates the order in which shafts are raised.

When the shafts move to give us a shed, the ends that are threaded through the heddles on these shafts are raised. The shuttle flies through with the weft thread, the shed is changed, and another set of ends if raised. As this series of steps is repeated, a pattern come into being – the pattern planned by you beforehand and achieved by working the treadles or levers. This is called a 'loom-controlled' weave.

When you work at a frame loom or a 2-shaft loom, both of which give only 2 sheds, you can change your fabric by laying in weft yarn in a design or by winding knots around the warp ends. These and other such techniques where the ends are picked up individually or in groups are 'finger-manipulated' weaves and usually are not indicated on drafts except when planning an overall design.

WEAVE DRAFT AND WEAVES

The Three Basic Weaves Are: Plain, Twill, Satin

From these, all weaves are derived. By combining parts of the basic weaves, or by combining two entire basic weaves, completely new patterns can evolve. This is the exciting part of weaving, so take the time to experiment with some combinations and see what interesting and beautiful patterns you can create.

PLAIN WEAVE

Of the loom-controlled weaves, the most basic is the *plain weave*, commonly called the *tabby weave*. We come upon this weave everyday in handkerchiefs, ginghams, taffeta fabrics and bed linens.

Plain weave is like darning. The weft goes over one warp end and under one and repeats across the width of the fabric. In the next row the weft alternates and goes under the end it had gone over and over the end it had gone under. The third row repeats the first and so we realize that this weave repeats on two weft picks. (For 'pick', see Glossary.)

The progression of a weave from draft to finished cloth

(1) WEAVE DRAFT   (2) ON THE LOOM
(3) FINISHED CLOTH

If we look at the weave draft above, we see that end No 3 is in the same position as end No 1 and end No 4 is in the same position as end No 2. Therefore, we know the plain weave repeats every two ends. As can be seen on graph paper, a draft is an exact reproduction of what happens to the weave on the loom.

NOTE The horizontal spaces in a *weave draft* represent the weft and the vertical spaces the warp.

When a square is blocked in, or x'd in, the weft thread goes under the warp end. If the square is blank, the weft goes over the warp end.

Plain weave can be made on a 4-, 8-, or even a 16-shaft loom as long as all odd ends are always raised on one shed and all even ends are always raised on the other shed. Only the plain weave can be done easily on a frame loom or a 2-shaft loom since there are just two shed possibilities.

VARIATIONS ON THE PLAIN WEAVE

Vertical stripes Different colours in the warp.
Horizontal stripes Different colours in the weft.
Irregular sleying Wide spaces between some ends or groups of ends crammed together.
Varied textures Textured yarn in warp or weft, or both.
Weft-faced fabric Weft completely or almost completely covers the warp. Tapestry weave is an example of this. There are fewer ends than picks per centimetre.
Irregular threading pattern This is explained in the threading section on page 47.
Modified basket weave Put two picks of weft instead of one in every shed.
Finger-manipulated weaves
If you want more changes in pattern by way of more sheds, then you will need a loom that provides more sheds. For a beginner, a 4-shaft loom offers more than enough possibilities for exploration, so we will limit our discussion to this. Keep in mind that whatever is possible on a 4-shaft loom is also possible on 8, 12, or 16 shafts.

TWILL WEAVE

The second basic weave, the twill, is very popular and has many variations. An even-balanced weave is produced when there is an equal number of picks and warp ends per centimetre. The simple diagonal effect in the twill weave makes it especially desirable for suiting and other clothing fabrics.

This weave repeats on 4 ends and 4 picks and should be made on a 4-shaft loom. A balanced twill (two shafts up and two down) is written $\frac{2}{2}$. Twills run either to the right or to the left; I have concentrated on the left-handed twills in this book.

Left-handed twill – **(A)** one repeat, **(B)** two repeats in warp and weft.

VARIATIONS ON TWILL WEAVE

Weft-faced twill
The warp is almost completely
covered. It is written $\frac{1}{3}$.
2 repeats

Warp-faced twill
The filling is almost completely
covered. It is written $\frac{3}{1}$.
2 repeats.

Broken twill
The same weave but not woven
in consecutive order.
The diagonal line of the
weave is 'broken' so as
to achieve a textured all-over
effect. 2 repeats

Waved twill
A zigzag line is formed when
the weave is reversed at the
end of 4 picks and runs to
the right for 2 picks. 2 repeats

In addition to these variations, completely different looks can be given to the twill weave by a multi-coloured warp and weft and the use of textured yarns. There are countless other variations possible in the weave itself – diamond patterns, triangular patterns; this is an area where you can experiment with much satisfaction.

SATIN WEAVE

If you want a cloth with a smooth, lustrous surface, the satin weave is the answer to your search. This is the third basic weave and in order for it to be a 'true' satin, it needs at least 5 shafts for one repeat. However, a mock, or irregular, satin can be constructed on a 4-shaft loom. The one drafted below, in 2 repeats, is called a 'crow' or 'swansdown' weave.

'CROW' SATIN

A satin weave is usually used when you wish to bring either the warp or the weft to the surface without having a set pattern to the weave. The 'crow' weave above would bring up the weft and hide most of the warp. If you wish to do the reverse, the weave would appear as shown below.

SOME COMMON WEAVES AND DRAFTS FOR A 4-SHAFT LOOM

PLAIN WEAVE

MODIFIED BASKET WEAVE

(1) Plain weave draft shows two repeats in weft and in warp

(2) Modified basket weave. Weave draft shows two repeats in warp and weft

TWILL WEAVE

BASKET WEAVE

(3) Left-handed twill weave. Weave draft shows two repeats in warp and weft

(4) Basket weave. Weave draft shows two repeats in warp and weft

'CROW' WEAVE

'CROW' WEAVE

(5) 'Crow' satin weave, an irregular weft-faced weave. Weave draft shows two repeats in warp and weft

(6) 'Crow' satin weave, an irregular warp-faced weave. Weave draft shows two repeats in warp and weft

WARP PLAN

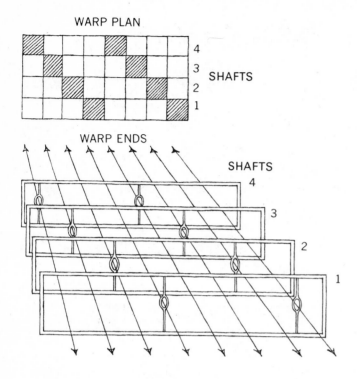

SHAFTS

WARP ENDS

SHAFTS

THREADING ACCORDING TO WARP PLAN

LAMS
ATTACHED TO
SHAFTS

PLAIN
WEAVE
TIE-UP

TREADLES

6 5 4 3 2 1

The warp plan and lifting plan
as translated on the loom

Knot used for connecting
lams to treadles

WARP PLAN

In order to see our weave realized the way we had created it, we must be sure the warp is threaded through the heddles correctly. This brings us to the warp plan. As before, every vertical space in the graph paper is a warp end, but now every horizontal space is a shaft. The shafts on the loom are numbered from front to back; on paper, from the bottom up, unless otherwise indicated.

Straight Draft (Straight Threading)

The warp plan that will give us any of the weaves already illustrated is the *straight draft*. Two repeats of a 4-shaft straight threading are shown left, as drafted on graph paper, and as threaded through the heddles. The repeats are in the width of the warp since there is as yet no weft.

To translate the straight draft, start with the lower right-hand corner. The first square on shaft No 1 is filled in. This means the first end on the right goes through a heddle on the first shaft. Continuing to the left we find an empty square on shaft No 1 but a filled-in one directly above on shaft No 2. This means the second warp end goes through a heddle on the second shaft. The third warp end then goes through a heddle on the third shaft and the fourth end on the fourth shaft. The fifth end is on shaft No 1 and begins the second repeat. The unit of repeat in a 4-shaft straight draft is four ends, which means that every fourth end will be woven alike.

No warp end goes through more than one heddle and the filled-in square in the draft means one warp end threaded through one heddle on one shaft.

Treadles are tied to lams according to the lifting plan. Lams are levers that lie between treadles and shafts and are numbered according to the shafts they are tied to. Pressing on the treadles pulls on the lams which in turn raises or lowers the shafts. The treadles have been numbered from right to left.

Treadle No 2 is tied to shaft No 1 and No 3. Treadle No 4 is tied to shafts No 2 and No 4. This tie-up is for plain weave.

This is the most common warp plan and can be done

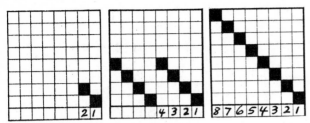

Straight draft shown on two, four and eight shafts. Numbers below drafts refer to shafts.

on any number of shafts from 12 to 16. The warp ends are pulled through consecutive shaft heddles and, on graph paper, the threading forms a diagonal line.

Irregular Threading

On a 2-shaft loom this draw produces only a plain weave. In order to achieve different weave effects, you would have to design an irregular threading pattern, such as the one below. Using this threading, the weave repeats on 12 ends and, if there is a pick used in each shed, on 2 picks, and looks exactly like the drawing-in draft.

A 2-shaft warp plan in an irregular threading pattern

Point Draft (Waved Draft)

Another fairly common warp plan is the *point*. The unit of repeat, if used on a 4-shaft loom, is 6 ends. The fifth end is no longer on shaft No 1, as in the straight draft, but on No 3. The sixth end is on shaft No 2. This draft used with the even-balanced or the reverse twill produces the patterns shown at below right. These are known as 'rose path' variations.

By studying the warp plan and weave draft below right, you can see that wherever the same shaft occurs, the weave over it remains the same. For example, follow the weave up the paper wherever it falls on shaft No. 2. You will see it is always two filled-in squares, followed by three empty squares, then three filled-in squares, then three empty ones, ending with one filled-in square. This is so because every time a shaft is raised, all warp ends threaded through that shaft must also be raised. All ends threaded through shaft No 2 heddles will raise and weave the same throughout the width of the warp. All ends on shaft No 1 will weave whenever that shaft is raised, all those on shaft No 3 will weave whenever that one is raised, and all those on shaft No 4 will weave when that shaft is raised.

The shaft numbers are at the bottom of the warp plan. Please keep in mind that the weaves show 2 repeats in the warp and weft.

'ROSE PATH' — TWO VARIATIONS

The $\frac{2}{2}$ twill weave (*right*) drafted over the even point draw. The numbers on the side indicate the lifting plan. The $\frac{2}{2}$ reverse twill weave (*far right*) over the even point draw. Two repeats are shown in weft and warp

A 4-shaft point or waved draft showing two repeats

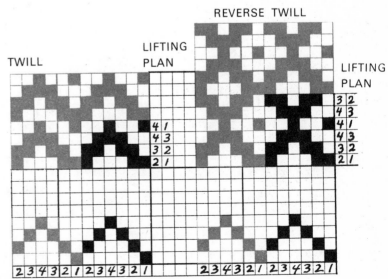

SHAFT NO

LIFTING PLAN

All that is lacking now is a plan to tell you which shafts to raise and in what order. This plan is called the lifting plan. We can figure out the lifting plan from one repeat of the weave. The vertical spaces indicate a shaft and the horizontal spaces the weft. On a 4-shaft loom our lifting plan will never be any wider than four spaces.

For the plain weave, the plan reads as below:

On a floor loom, the tie-ups of the treadles are:

2-shaft loom – First shed, treadle No 1 tied to shaft No 1.
Second shed, treadle No 2 tied to shaft No 2.
4-shaft loom – First shed, treadle No 1 tied to shafts No 1 and No 3.
Second shed, treadle No 2 tied to shafts No 2 and No 4.

On a table loom, the following levers must be pressed:

2-shaft loom – First shed, lever raising shaft No 1.
Second shed, lever raising shaft No 2.
4-shaft loom – First shed, levers raising shafts No 1 and No 3.
Second shed, levers raising shafts No 2 and No 4.

In the following two patterns, I have used x's for the warp plan and lifting plan, so that it can be seen at a glance that these two drafts are not part of the weave draft.

PATTERN No 1

Commonly called 'goose-eye', this pattern belongs to the twill family of weaves. There are 2 repeats shown in the warp and 1 in the weft. Study the numbers on the side of the lifting plan. On the first pick only one shaft is raised in order to obtain the weave. Follow the lifting plan upwards, and you will see that for every pick only one shaft has to be raised. On the table loom just follow the numbers upwards and press the lever connected to the shaft desired for that pick.

On a floor loom there are a limited number of treadles, usually six for a 4-shaft loom. Be sure that every number, or combination of numbers, found in the lifting plan is connected to a treadle. This is known

as the tie-up. In pattern No 1, there are four different numbers, each attached to a separate treadle and pressed according to the way it falls in the lifting plan. Study the numbers on the lifting plan and on the warp plan more closely. You will see that they read upwards in the same sequence as they do from right to left. When this occurs in a draft, it is to be 'woven, or treadled, as drawn-in'. In this instance the lifting plan is not necessary since the pattern can be achieved by simply following the shaft order from right to left.

Please note that should you decide to change your lifting plan and press the first eight numbers and then repeat them, you will no longer have the goose-eye, but a type of herringbone weave.

PATTERN No 2

'M's and O's' is an attractive texture weave. For this pattern two shafts are attached on every treadle. In all, there are four different number combinations. Attach four treadles to the four combinations. The middle row of numbers is the actual treadle number that is pressed. The row of numbers on the far right is a further shortening of the instructions and indicates that each combination of treadles must be pressed twice.

Some weavers prefer to have each treadle attached to a different shaft and then use both feet to press two treadles. In this case, the treadles are used exactly as the levers on the table loom.

NOTE The drafts I show throughout are designed for the rising shed loom. For a loom with a sinking shed, reverse the draft indications so that the empty squares for the rising shed loom become the filled-in squares for the sinking shed loom, and *vice versa*. After the weave draft is adjusted, plot the lifting plan accordingly. Be careful of the weft-faced and warp-faced weaves because they need the whole shaft lowering or raising, respectively, to obtain a good shed on a counterbalanced loom.

As I mentioned earlier, methods of writing drafts differ from school to school, from teacher to teacher, and from place to place. If you don't find drafts exactly as they are given in this book, don't be dismayed. As long as a draft contains the following information it will not be difficult to translate:

1. The number of shafts the weave needs in order to be reproduced.
2. How to thread the loom for the desired weave.
3. What shafts to raise and in what order. Remember that a filled-in square indicates a shaft must be raised.

With these points in mind, you will soon become quite adept at translating drafts and will join in the weaver's common treasure hunt – that of finding new drafts and adapting them to your needs and loom.

PATTERN NO 1 'Goose-Eye', a weft-faced weave based on a $\frac{1}{3}$ twill   LIFTING PLAN

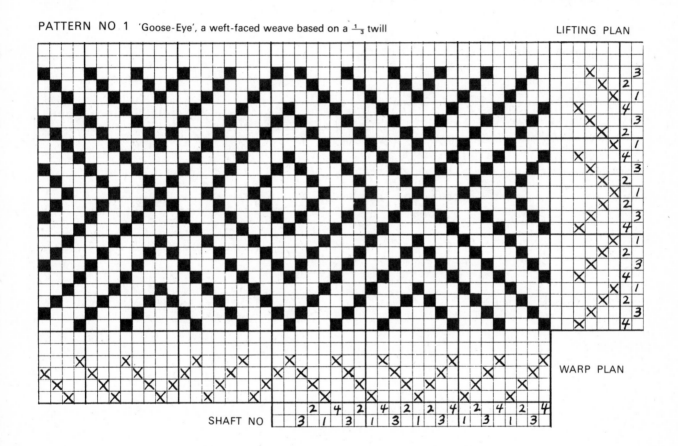

WARP PLAN

SHAFT NO

PATTERN NO 2
'M's and O's' showing a complete lifting plan and (far right) its abbreviated version

LIFTING
PLAN TREADLES

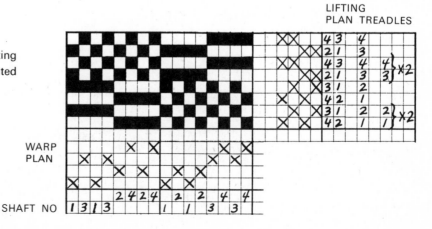

WARP PLAN

SHAFT NO

STARTING TO WEAVE

The time has finally come when you are seated in front of the loom ready to weave. No matter how long or extensive your weaving career becomes, there will always be this thrill the moment you sit at the loom, open the first shed, throw the shuttle and begin another lovely rug, fabric or wall hanging. If it has seemed a long time to get here, this is only natural; the preparation of the second warp will go quicker, the third even faster, and you will gain more speed with each successive warp. Also, as you become more experienced, you will realize that these tasks are important parts of the weaving craft, and you will get pleasure from doing them successfully.

Now, let us move on to the actual weaving – how to do it, pitfalls to avoid, and errors that can be corrected.

WEAVING ON THE 4-SHAFT LOOM

The Heading

When the warp is tied in bundles around the front apron bar (see pages 36–7, Beaming and Threading the Loom), spaces occur at certain intervals. By weaving a 2·5 to 5 cm (1 to 2 in.) heading, these spaces will be closed and the warp will lie in a straight line from the reed to the point of weaving. The smaller the individual bundle, the narrower the heading used. The heading should be of heavy yarn, string or rags (preferably in a colour contrasting to the weft),

The warp is shown tied to the front apron bar. The heading is woven in to spread out the bundles

in order to spread the bundles quickly and not to waste the warp. The heading yarn is wound in butterflies or on a stick shuttle and beaten down quite heavily.

Open Shed No 1

Press the treadle or lever and open shed No 1. Pass the shuttle through from right to left, allowing the weft thread to remain behind in the shed, extending about 5 cm (2 in.) outside the right selvedge.

Beginning to weave after the heading has been put in

If you are using the boat shuttle, hold it in your right hand between thumb and middle finger. A sharp forward thrust of the index finger should provide the force needed to land the shuttle on the left edge of the weaving.

The shuttle glides on the taut warp ends that form the underside of the shed. The weft thread should be left in the shed at an angle – the lowest point where the thread enters and the highest where it exits. If it is left lying in a straight line, a taut, pulled-in

CROSS SECTION
OF WARP AND WEFT

The weft is placed in the shed on a diagonal so that the yarn has enough slack to interlace with the warp ends, avoiding a pulled-in line

An even selvedge (*left*) with the weft turned correctly around the selvedge ends. An uneven selvedge (*right*) caused by turning the weft too loosely or too tightly

line will result since there would not be enough 'give' in the yarn to interlace with the warp.

Using the Beater

Grasp the top of the beater firmly in the centre so that the pressure of the beat is spread evenly along the weft as it is pushed down into the warp. If you handle the beater more to one side than the other, you will find your web growing larger at a slant. Pull the beater forward with a swift, sharp movement.

Change to Shed No 2

Return the beater to its original position and change to shed No 2. Beat down once more. The force of the beat depends on the temperament of the weaver, the type of fabric being woven and the feeling for the beat that a weaver develops. Some weavers have a heavy beat and it is difficult for them to adapt themselves to doing very loose fabrics. Of others the reverse is true, and they tap lightly instead of beating firmly. You will find that your beat can change with your mood. On a day when you are mad at the world, the beat tends to be firm and aggressive. On days of peace and quiet, the touch is apt to be lighter. Ideally, the beat should be a firm but controlled movement so that the picks per centimetre will be even throughout the entire woven piece.

Consider the Selvedge

After the second beat, pass the shuttle from left to right, leaving the weft thread snugly around

the left selvedge. Maintain an even selvedge – the weft should not hang out beyond in a loop nor should it pull in tightly. There will be a normal amount of draw-in from selvedge to selvedge, but anything beyond this should be avoided since some of these pulled-in selvedge ends could be cut by the beater.

Inspect Warp and Make Necessary Adjustments

Continue weaving in this manner until the bundles are properly spaced. During this time any mistakes in drawing-in or sleying should be corrected and uneven tension remedied.

Warp end threaded incorrectly If the mistake is in the drawing-in, the warp end must be removed

The dotted line indicates a warp end being drawn through a heddle left empty because of incorrect threading

from the bundle and redrawn correctly. If the shaft does not have an empty heddle to accommodate the misplaced warp end, tie a makeshift string heddle onto the shaft bars.

Missing warp end If there is a missing warp end, this can be corrected by making a string heddle on the necessary shaft and inserting a warp end of the length needed. One side of this new warp end is tied in the bundle and the other around a spool that is allowed to hang from the back of the loom. Weight the spool so that the new end will have the same tension as the rest of the warp. Resley the ends in the reed to accommodate this new end.

Extra warp end If there is an extra warp end, remove it and resley the reed correctly. If this leaves the heddle without a warp end running through it, it will not interfere with either the weaving or the spacing of the warp.

Incorrect sleying Warp ends are sometimes twisted behind the reed by incorrect sleying. Remove the guilty ends from the bundle and pull them out of the reed. Untwist and resley correctly. If there is a skipped dent or too many ends per dent, resley that section of the warp so affected.

As all this illustrates, it is better to take the time to check back every 5 or 7·5 cm (2 or 3 in.) while drawing-in and sleying instead of having to take even more time to correct these errors later.

The above shows how warp ends can become twisted when incorrectly sleyed

Uneven tension A wavy line in the weft means uneven tension. The bundles must be retied at the points where the tension is not correct.

Wavy lines in the weft caused by uneven tension in the warp. The tension must be corrected

Finish Off Heading

As soon as spaces are closed and mistakes corrected, cut the heading thread from the shuttle so that it extends about 2·5 cm (1 in.) beyond the selvedge. This heading will prevent unravelling when the project is finished and taken off the loom. Also, a few picks of the heading can be put in at the end of the project until you decide how you want to finish it off, whether by knots, fringes, hemming or stitching by either hand or machine. If you are doing plain weave, you should end the heading on the second shed.

Tuck in the new weft yarn that extends beyond the right selvedge and bring it to the back of the weaving

The Weft

Take your shuttle with the weft yarn and begin exactly as you did for the heading except that, when you open the second shed, insert the yarn that had been left to extend beyond the right selvedge. In the heading it was not important to tuck in the beginning and end of the yarn, but in the project itself the ends must be brought back into the warp and out on the wrong side.

Piecing the Yarn

When you start a new bobbin of the same thread, you can 'piece' the yarn by laying the new thread beside the old one. Make sure they overlap for about 3·75 cm (1½ in.), then beat into position.

Piecing the weft threads by laying the new thread over the old one in the same shed

Weaving with Two Colours

If you are weaving with two different colours and the colour repeat is small, it is not necessary to cut

When weaving with two colours, the colour not in use is carried along the selvedge until used again. This is a method for narrow colour repeats. Note the start of the weft thread tucked back into shed

the thread with every colour change. When you finish with colour No 1, lay the shuttle aside, allowing the thread to hang loosely from the fabric. Pick up colour No 2 shuttle and continue to weave. Every time you are on the same side as colour No 1, go under it with the No 2 shuttle and bring it alongside the selvedge as illustrated below left.

Bringing the Warp Forward

Continue weaving as long as the shed opening is wide enough to accommodate the shuttle and the beater has enough space in which to beat down. When this is no longer possible, slowly release the back ratchet so that a small supply of warp can be brought to the weaving position. Roll the fabric around the cloth beam until the last pick woven is as far as it can be from the reed but can still be reached by the beater. If necessary, release a bit more warp from the warp beam. Then secure the ratchets, adjust the tension until it is taut enough and continue weaving.

If you have released too much warp, rewind the excess back onto the warp beam.

Broken Warp End

To replace a broken warp end, measure out a new end the length of the warp yet to be woven, plus 10 to 15·25 cm (4 to 6 in.). Tie it in a bowknot to the broken end at the back of the loom. Remove the broken end from the dent and heddle, thread the new end through in its place allowing it to overlap the web by about 10 cm (4 in.). Secure the front of the new end around a straight pin inserted into the web about 2·5 or 5 cm (1 or 2 in.) forward from the last pick. Untie the bowknot and pull the new end until it has the same tension as the rest of the warp, then retie.

As the weaving progresses and the warp moves forward, the bowknot will come closer to the back shaft. You must watch for this and untie it when it gets too close. Then retie it at the slabstock.

When the project is finished, pull all broken ends and new ends through to the back of the weaving with a darning needle and trim.

BROKEN END TIED
AT BACK OF LOOM

CLOSE-UP OF
PIN IN WEB

To replace a broken warp end, tie the new end to the broken end at the back of the loom. It is then secured at the front of the loom around a pin inserted into the web

Measuring the Weave

Have a tape measure handy to keep track of how much you have woven and to make sure your picks per cm are constant. Insert a pin or loop a piece of yarn around the selvedge every time you have measured the length.

2.54 cm

Measuring the number of picks per centimetre with a tape measure

To Remove the Weaving

At the end of your weaving, cut the project off and untie or cut it from the front apron bar, allowing enough unwoven warp ends to remain for the finishing. As mentioned earlier, heavy weft can be woven in for about 2·5 cm (1 in.) at the end of the project.

To Tie a New Warp

If you plan to use the same warp plan and sleying arrangement on your next warp, then cut the warp in front of the beater. Tie it in slipknots so it will not be pulled out of the reed and heddles. The new warp can then be tied onto the remaining warp.

To tie a new warp to an old one, place the warp chain, with lease sticks in the cross, in front of the beater. Secure the lease sticks in position and cut the loop end of the new warp. Tie the ends in consecutive order to the old warp. When all the ends have been tied, work the knots slowly through the reed, then through the heddles. Be sure to roll back the slack that will exist between the beater and shafts. Continue beaming as explained on pages 36–7.

NOTE The important processes of weaving can be broken down into four basic steps.

1. Open the shed.
2. Beat the previous weft.
3. Pass the shuttle through shed carrying the new weft pick.
4. Beat new pick into position.

The goals to strive for in weaving are an even beat and even selvedges.

WEAVING ON THE FRAME LOOM

Weaving on the frame loom is a very simple process but not a fast one since making the two sheds requires more handwork than on a table or floor loom. However, because the hands are so involved with the warp, a comfortable intimacy and rapport develop between the weaver and his work.

Making the First Shed

Make the chain spacer (see page 39). Open the first shed with the shed stick and insert weft. The weft can be carried on a small stick shuttle (good to use when one colour is carried from selvedge to selvedge), flute, bobbin or butterfly (see pages 40–41). Do not pull the weft through tightly but leave it in the shed at a diagonal. Close shed.

Beat down weft with short sharp taps starting from the side you entered. A tapestry comb or table fork can be used for this.

SHED NO 1

Making the Second Shed – Method No 1

There are two ways to open the second shed. One is to pull the string heddles down and out towards yourself, thereby lifting the even-numbered warp ends. However, since it is possible to grasp only a limited amount of heddles in your hand, you must work your way across the warp in sections. I usually proceed from right to left. The left hand pulls on the heddles as the right hand inserts the weft, pushing it from one open section to the other until the left selvedge is reached. Beat down as for first shed.

SHED NO 2

Making the Second Shed – Method No 2

This is probably the easiest method when you want one weft colour across the entire warp. Unscrew and lift heddle rod. It in turn lifts all the even-numbered warp ends. Have a second shed stick at hand and insert it into the opening. If the opening is too small to allow this, push your original shed stick to the top of the loom as far as it will go. Insert the second stick and release heddle rod. Open shed and insert weft. Remove stick and beat down. The stick can be used to push down the weft, but the comb must be used to

FRAME LOOM

beat down firmly. Check that all even-numbered ends have been lifted.

Moving the Warp Down

When you have woven as close as possible to the heddle rod and no longer have a wide comfortable shed, remove one of the front tension sticks. Then push up on the warp-end and revolve the woven warp slowly around the bottom of the frame. Stop when the last pick woven is about 5 cm (2 in.) from the top of the bottom frame.

Keeping Selvedges Even

At times it will be difficult to keep selvedges even and the woven piece from narrowing. To remedy both problems thread a tapestry needle with warp thread and run the thread through the selvedges every 5 or 7·5 cm (2 or 3 in.). Tie the thread around the frame sides, making sure it is taut enough to keep the weaving spread to its intended width. As the warp revolves, these threads are pushed down the sides or cut.

At Completion

When the project is completed, cut the warp off at the warp-end bar, remove the chain spacer and finish off the piece as you had planned.

NOTE The process of weaving on the frame loom can be broken down into four steps.
1. Open shed No. 1 (odd-numbered ends) with shed stick; insert weft.
2. Close shed and beat down weft.
3. Open shed No. 2 (even-numbered ends) by working heddle strings; insert weft.
4. Close shed and beat down weft.

Table mat woven of strips of velvet, satin, and yarn in plain weave with the soumak stitch. If the sides are joined, this becomes an accessory bag

STARTING TO WEAVE

ACCESSORY BAG OR TABLE MAT

Plain Weave with Soumak Stitch

I am sure that in your home you have many pieces of fabric – clothing, drapery, towels or remnants left over from sewing – that you are about to throw out. Don't, for these fabrics, cut into strips, can provide us with the weft for our first project – an accessory bag. This bag will carry the yarn, bobbins, scissors and other tools that you will accumulate in your weaving life. It can be used also as a shopping bag or, if the selvedges are very straight, you can piece two or three lengths together to make a small rug.

In this project, we will be concerned mostly with the first basic weave, the plain weave (see pages 42–3), and a novelty technique called 'soumak'. Soumak is a finger-manipulated weave, which means that even on a table or floor loom it must be put in by hand and not by the raising or lowering of shafts. It is an Oriental carpet tapestry weave and produces a raised diagonal effect which is a way to achieve surface interest in a two-shed loom.

Accessory bag with leather thong handles. It is a useful carry-all for holding weaving utensils. Instructions on following page

Felt strips instead of rags were used by H. G. Kargus to make this attractive rug

Unique carry-all bag, using twine, jute and string, made by Ahza Cohen

MATERIALS NEEDED

Warp 8/4 cotton carpet warp, about 156 m (160 yds).
Weft $\frac{1}{2}$ to 1 kg (1 to 2 lb) of cloth cut into 2·5 cm (1 in.) wide strips and pieced together, as shown, so that you have a continuous strip with which to weave. The cloth may be of any fibre content, but I generally try to keep all shrinkables together in one project and non-shrinkables in another. In the bag illustrated here, I used taffeta from an old evening dress, velvet from an old blouse, and corduroy and cotton from my sewing scrap basket. Also have lengths of heavy yarn to use in the soumak sections.

Piece the rags at right angles prior to winding them on shuttles. The seam is trimmed to eliminate bulk in the material

CALCULATIONS

Sett 4 ends per cm (10 per in.). Double last two ends on each side for selvedge. Total number of ends, 104.
Width on loom 25 cm (10 in.).
Length For *frame loom*, a continuous warp around the entire loom (see pages 38–9); for *table or floor loom*, dressed length is 1·5 m (1½ yds).
Finished length 60 cm (24 in.).

WARP PLAN

For a floor or table loom, thread on a straight draw (page 46) and follow the directions on page 48 for the making of two sheds. Directions for the frame are on page 55.

TECHNIQUES

Soumak Stitch

Plain weave is used throughout except in areas indicated as soumak. Soumak is made as follows:

1. Weave a row of plain weave, from right to left.

A right to left slant of soumak stitch is shown in 2nd row of dark weft. Reverse slant is seen in unfinished row

This is the beginning of the yarn section so you should have the beginning of this pick extending beyond the selvedge at the right. Tuck in the extended yarn on the right in the same shed.

2. Have the warp in a neutral position (a closed shed). Count in 6 ends from the left and insert shuttle front to back between the 6th and 7th ends.

3. Bring shuttle back to surface by inserting it, back to front, 2 ends to the left between the 4th and 5th ends, *over* the surface weft.

4. Count over 6 ends from this new position and repeat as in No 3 and No 4.

5. Continue in this manner across the width of the warp.

6. Beat the weft into place and weave a pick of plain weave going right to left.

7. Begin a second row of soumak as above, *except* this time when you go under the 2 ends bring the shuttle to the surface *under* the weft yarn already on the surface. This will change the slant of the stitch.

Soumak can have many variations. It can be brought over 2, 3, 4 or 5 ends instead of 6. This depends on the sett, since too long a float is not desirable. There can be many rows of plain weave in between the soumak rows, but at least one row is needed to bind down the soumak. The soumak does not have to extend across the entire row, but can be used instead as a random effect or to achieve a motif. If you pull tightly on the 2 enclosed ends, gaps may occur in the warp. For the purpose of this project, it is advisable not to pull this tightly and to concentrate instead on keeping the threads aligned.

DESIGN

I have used a random stripe pattern determined by the amount of strips I had in each of the various fabrics. Since the fibre content of the fabrics was almost all different, I strove for unity through colour, choosing only those fabrics that looked well together. If you have an odd assortment that seems to have no colour unity, try dyeing them all with the same colour. The colours will still be different, but they should have a common glow. Naturally, the effectiveness of this depends on the fibre content of your cloth. For information on how to dye, see page 24.

Pick your fabrics with a thought for textural contrasts and remember you can use scraps of yarn for the soumak or for the fine stripes.

HELPFUL HINTS

1. After you have cut and stitched the strips, wind each colour around a stick shuttle, attaching the strip by a slip knot around the arm of the shuttle. Do not try to handle lengths of more than 7·5 m (10 yds) at a time or the shuttle will become bulky and unwieldy.

2. Use a firm beat but do not expect the warp to be covered completely. Plan, therefore, on having the warp colour show and choose its colour in accordance with the weft you have on hand.

3. A heading, woven of yarn, can be made at the beginning and end of the project. It should be about 3·75 cm (1½ in.) wide and not beaten in very firmly since it should be pliable enough to be folded back as the hem. Fringe the project if a hem is not used. You should allow at least 10 cm (4 in.) of warp for the fringing but trim to about 5 cm (2 in.) after the fringe is made.

4. Be sure that the joining seams in the strips are folded towards the inside so they do not show. Also,

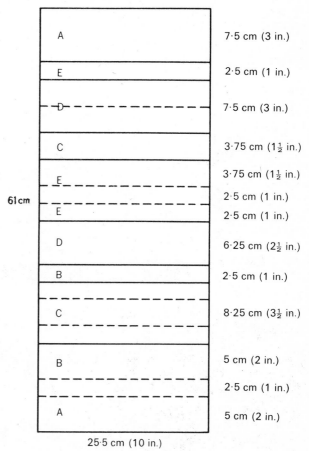

PATTERN FOR ACCESSORY BAG

A	7·5 cm (3 in.)
E	2·5 cm (1 in.)
D	7·5 cm (3 in.)
C	3·75 cm (1½ in.)
E	3·75 cm (1½ in.)
E	2·5 cm (1 in.)
E	2·5 cm (1 in.)
D	6·25 cm (2½ in.)
B	2·5 cm (1 in.)
C	8·25 cm (3½ in.)
B	5 cm (2 in.)
	2·5 cm (1 in.)
A	5 cm (2 in.)

61 cm

25·5 cm (10 in.)

KEY:
Dotted lines – one row of soumak stitch
Grey areas – solid soumak
Numbers – width of stripes
Letters – arrangement of colours

all fabrics that have a right and wrong side, like napped fabrics, should be folded and beaten in to show the right side to advantage. When starting a new colour, taper the ends of both rag strips to be joined so that the overlapping will not be thick and create a hump.

FINISHING

1. Trim the back side of the project.

2. Put wrong sides of bag together and sew seams.

3. Braid a handle for your bag, using heavy yarn, or attach leather thong strips in any length you want.

RYA RUG

Plain Weave with Rug Knots

One of the most luxuriant and decorative pieces you can have in your home is a rya rug. The rya rug has a thick pile about 4 to 5 cm (1½ to 2 in.) high that adds depth to the colours used.

These rugs come to us from Scandinavia where in olden days their deep pile was necessary for warmth on board ships during winter sealing and fishing trips and as 'throws' in sleighs. They were used as coverings on beds and were hung on walls and placed on floors for added protection against the cold.

As they became less of a practical necessity, their patterns became more ornamental and colourful. Today the designing and making of rya rugs is considered an art form.

The rug consists of warp, weft, and the Ghiordes knot. This knot has been used in Oriental carpeting since the 14th century. It is wound around two warp ends. Oriental rugs, which have a very short pile, have between 12 to 50 knots per sq cm (80 to 320 per sq in.) and a minimum of weft shots to hold the pile in place. Our rya adaptation will have only 12 to 15 knots per sq cm (8 to 10 per sq in.) and, because of the height of the pile, about 2 cm (¾ in.) of weft between each row of knots.

Our rug will be made in 25-cm (10-in.) squares, woven separately, then sewn together. Narrow looms or frame looms can accommodate this size easily. But the size is quite flexible; if you make approximately a 1·80 × 1·20 m (6 ft × 4 ft) now and decide to change the size later, you do so by simply removing squares or weaving additional ones.

If you should want to make one or two experimental squares, they can always be used as ornamental pieces of colour on the wall or on footstools or as cushion covers. The underside of the cushion can be canvas or plain weave.

(*Opposite*) 'Chartres', a hand-knotted rya rug 1·525 m × 1·825 m (5 ft by 6 ft) with a 5 cm (2 in.) pile. The design was inspired by the stained glass windows of that cathedral

MATERIALS NEEDED

Overall size of rug This is a matter of personal preference. A good area rug size is 1·80 m × 1·20 m (6 ft × 4 ft). The nearest size to this, using our 25-cm square, would be 1·75 m × 1·25 m (approx 70 in. × 50 in.).

Warp 8/4 cotton carpet warp. A rug 7 squares by 5 squares, or 1·75 m × 1·25 m (70 in. × 50 in.) requires about 3,600 m (3,900 yds). One 25-cm (10-in.) square made on a 50 cm × 40 cm (20 in. × 16 in.) frame loom requires about 100 m (110 yds). If you are doing this on a floor or table loom, you can make a longer warp and do several samples on one warp. At least 4 squares could be woven on a 2·75 m (3-yd) warp; in that case you will need 240 m (280 yds) for each warp. The colour of the warp is not important since it will be completely covered by the weft. Linen warp yarn can be used, but it is somewhat more expensive.

Weft 3- or 4-ply wool rug yarn or heavy cotton rug filler. About 2·25 kg (5 lb), in a colour to go with the pile, are needed for a rug 7 squares by 5 squares. A soft twist yarn covers the warp more easily than a hard twist. Weaving the ground goes quicker with a heavy yarn but, in some cases of very heavy yarn, parts of the warp will remain exposed. I prefer to cover the warp completely, but since this is the underside of the rug, it is really your choice as to whether or not you want the warp exposed.

Pile Plan to use a total of about 405 kg (10 lb) of rug wool. In the two designs illustrated here, there are predominantly two colours equally divided, requiring about 2·25 kg (5 lb) each. However, you will notice I

A 25 cm (10 in.) square of the rya rug made on the frame loom showing back and front. Notice the Swedish braid (see page 65) on two sides of square at left

did not use just one colour in an area, but three or four shades of one colour in the 3- or 4-ply yarn. This gives a colour subtlety and interest that cannot be achieved with a single yarn of heavy rug weight.

Should you wish to have different shades of a colour, divide your poundage equally between them. I heartily recommend making one experimental square in your chosen colour scheme before ordering the complete amounts. You can use yarns that you have at home, even though they may have no colour unity. Try giving them a related hue by over-dyeing as mentioned on page 24.

There are 'rug yarns' specifically marked as such. These are generally what I use although I am a great believer in mixing rug yarns with others of different weight, fibre content, and texture. A bit of linen gives an added lustrous quality to a rug. A hard twist yarn, together with a soft twist, provides textural interest, as does a strand or two of fine yarn mixed with a heavier one.

CALCULATIONS

Sett 3 ends per cm (8 per in.). Double last 2 ends on each side for selvedge. Total number of ends, 92.
Width on loom 28 cm (11 in.).
Length For *frame loom*, a continuous warp; for *table or floor loom*, 40 cm (16 in.) for each square. Allow 25 cm (10 in.) for the square and about 7·5 cm (3 in.) at each end so that the cut warp can be braided back.

WARP PLAN

Thread on a straight draft (refer to page 47) for a table or floor loom. Use plain weave as the ground weave.

DESIGN

There are two design possibilities offered here for the rya rug. However, if you have an idea of your own that you want to try, the following instructions will help you prepare your design.

To Prepare Design

1. A colour sketch is not necessary if your design is simple, but I would advise having one if it is complex. The colour sketch should be in scale to the dimensions of your rug, but does not have to be full size.

2. Draw your design in outline and in full size. Use heavy wrapping paper or paper bags taped together.

3. Divide the pattern and colour sketch into 25-cm (10-in.) squares. Use these to check against the pattern during weaving.

4. Consider where you plan to use the rug and place the outline sketch there together with yarn or fabrics in the colours you plan to order. In this way you can study the effects of the yarns and colours in your room before any purchasing is done and without having to return unwanted material.

PATTERNS

To develop Pattern 1, draw a 25-cm (10-in.) square with a diagonal line running across it. Place this behind your weaving to be sure the design changes from a dark to light colour at the correct knots.

Pattern 2 is also drawn on a 25-cm square. Find the centre of the square and draw a 17·5-cm (7-in.) circle. (A child's compass can be used or a plate near to this size.) Put diagram behind weaving to be sure the colour changes come at the correct knots. The circle in your weaving will never be an exact circle but an impression of one, because of the length of the knots. It will, however, be a more interesting pattern.

NOTE If you have the facilities, both these patterns can be woven in a larger square size than 25 cm.

Colour

Your choice of colours depends on where you intend to use the rug. If the combinations shown here fit your colour schemes, use them. If not, let them be a guide to the colours you need.

Pattern 1 has a very dramatic contrast of colours. To follow this guide, choose a dark colour for the brown area and a light one for the gold area. If you like the pattern, but the contrast is too extreme for your room setting, choose either a lighter colour for the brown area or a darker colour for the gold area. But be careful not to get the two colours so close in value that you cannot see the difference between them. The colouring of this pattern is based on a difference in value.

Pattern 2 has its colouring based on a difference in hue. Choose colours of close values but not of the same colour family. The result is a much more subtle effect than Pattern 1. Should you want to make this more striking, try colours of vastly different values.

In Pattern 1, I worked from a deep value to a light value of one colour family. To make this gradation, I changed one strand in each knot to a lighter value as I knotted across the warp. For example, if one knot was made up of three strands of deep gold, the knot next to it would have two strands of deep gold and one of a lighter gold. Then the next knot would have only one strand of deep gold and two of lighter gold. It is not necessary, however, to change value with every knot.

Pattern 2 has three close shades of each colour. Unlike Pattern 1, they are not graded from dark to light but are combined in every other knot.

TECHNIQUES

Background Plain weave is used for the background of the rug; it should be an old friend from Project No 1. Now, however, it is made with yarn and completely covers the warp. Beat well, to hold the knots securely in place.

Preparing the pile The rya knot can be made in one of two ways:

Method No 1, Cut the yarn beforehand into 10-cm (4-in.) long pieces. To precut it, make a 10-cm wide gauge of heavy cardboard or wood and wind the yarn around the gauge. Slit the yarn at each edge of the gauge with a razor blade or sharp knife. This is a good

These diagrams suggest pattern possibilities for two simple geometric designs.

PATTERN No 1 – DIAGONAL MOTIF (Seen on page 64)

25 cm (10 in.)

25 cm (10 in.)

The diagonal motif can be arranged to form many patterns. The border pattern at right has diagonal squares at top and bottom only; the rest are solid. Thirty-five squares are needed, 7 in length and 5 in width

SMALL TRIANGLES   BORDER

The circle motif can be used in an alternated pattern or centred. Thirty-five squares are needed

PATTERN No 2 – CIRCULAR MOTIF (Seen on page 61)

ALTERNATED   CENTRED

JOINING RYA SQUARES

Rya rug consisting of six 25-cm (10-in.) squares in the diagonal motif. One square has been detached to illustrate how the rug is assembled

The same rug squares rearranged to form a different pattern. Innumerable designs are possible with the simple diagonal pattern

method to use if you change colours in the knots frequently. I usually have the yarn arranged around me with each colour in a small box; then I just pick up the colours I need for a knot and tie them around the warp. The strands of the yarn do not have to be exactly the same size, but there should be no difference greater than 2·5 cm (1 in.).

Method No 2 Make butterflies of the yarn and colours you plan to use together. As the butterfly goes

PILE GAUGES

Wind yarn around gauge; cut along groove in gauge to form pile

around the warp ends to form the knot, it goes also around a gauge on the surface of the rug. The gauge is 5 cm (2 in.) high and can be made of cardboard. It should be the length of your square. More elaborate

gauges can be made of metal or wood, with a slit on top so that a razor can glide over and cut the knot loops. With the cardboard gauge, the loops can be cut with scissors.

Ghiordes knot The knot is made over two warp ends. Working from left to right, the yarn goes down between two ends, then under the left end, up and over the left and right ends, under the right end, and up between the two ends. The two yarn ends meet in the centre and are pulled tightly forward and up.

If you are using a butterfly, the gauge is laid over the yarn; the butterfly goes over it and to the next set of warp ends for the next knot. As you make this knot,

Ghiordes knot shown after being cut. The next pick of plain weave will push down the knots and secure them firmly in the woven web

pull up tightly on the yarn, but not so tightly as to buckle the gauge. The gauge will stand on end when the yarn is tightened around it. Proceed to the end of your row or colour, always remembering to go under and over the gauge between each set of knotted warp ends.

STEPS IN CONSTRUCTION

1. Weave 2·5 cm (1 in.) of plain weave. Be sure you leave at least 5 cm (2 in.) of warp before the first pick. This will later be turned under and braided over the 2·5 cm of plain weave.

2. Tie a row of rya knots. The end selvedge threads, which are doubled (one doubled end on each side), are left without knots. The knots are made with the warp in a neutral position. If you are using the gauge, cut the knot loops and remove gauge.

3. Take the shuttle with the weft yarn and go twice around the empty end selvedge threads. Weave a pick of plain weave. Do not use the same shed that you wove in before the row of knots.

4. Change sheds. Go twice around the empty end selvedge threads on the other side of the square. Weave a pick of plain weave.

5. Continue with plain weave for 2 cm ($\frac{3}{4}$ in.).

6. Tie the second row of knots.

7. Repeat steps 3, 4 and 5 and continue in this manner for 10 rows of knots.

8. After you have finished the 10th row of knots, weave ·65 cm ($\frac{1}{4}$ in.) plain weave, making sure to beat extra hard to insure the knots against slipping out.

9. On the frame loom, measure up on the warp at least 5 cm (2 in.) and cut off the sample. On a long warp, on the floor or table loom, weave a piece of soft cardboard 5 cm wide in a shed of plain weave. In the alternate shed of plain weave, insert another 5 cm cardboard. This will give the needed lengths for the braid. You can now go on to the next square.

HELPFUL HINTS

1. Leave the weft yarn loose and at a diagonal in the shed before beating down. Otherwise, the selvedges will tend to pull in more than is allowed for. Strive for neat straight selvedges.

2. Put in more weft picks in the ground weave than necessary. Successive rows tend to beat down the

earlier rows so that you may end up with less than 2 cm ($\frac{3}{4}$ in.) between each row of knots.

FINISHING

1. Trim the back side of the square.

2. Braid the warp ends over the back of the square, using a *Swedish braid*. As you braid, push the strands of the braid with your thumb towards the square so that they will lie tightly against the square. Start at the back on the left and work over by twos. Take two ends and go under two, over two and under two. Bring the original two to the surface and point towards the top of the square. Take the next two ends at the left and work them under the next two, over and under and to the surface and point upwards. Do this with all the warp ends until you have four pairs left at the right. Braid these into a 4-strand braid about 2·5 cm (1 in.) long. Start from the left and tie the pairs of warp ends together so that you are assured of a firm edge when you sew the squares together.

3. Sew the squares together using a tapestry needle threaded with the same yarn or colour as the weft. The yarn should be about twice the length of one side of your square. Place the squares to be sewn according to your pattern. Attach the yarn securely to the lower right edge by looping it a couple of times around either the braid or the weft. Pull the needle through the loop on the lower left side. This loop is made by either the braid or weft, depending on which side of the square you are sewing. The needle is pulled up through the loop and across to the right side, where it is pushed down through the loop. Continue in this manner to the top of the squares. At the end of the seam, take two or three loops to finish off. The 2·5-cm (1-in.) braids can be sewn down at the same time or tacked down later with finer thread. Trim the warp ends when the seam is finished. The stitches of this seam can be spaced at about ·3 to ·65 cm ($\frac{1}{8}$ to $\frac{1}{4}$ in.) apart depending on the weight of your sewing yarn. Pull tightly enough so that the edges being sewn lie smoothly next to each other, but be careful not to overlap. One thing to watch for is that one of the squares does not shift while you are stitching or it will not match to the other square at the end of the seam.

(*Above*) Front of gold bag with tassels and braided handles. An example of the 'straight laid-in' technique. Here the turns are made on the face of the fabric to add textural effect to the design. (*Opposite, above*) Back of gold bag. Here the turns are made on the wrong side of the fabric, resulting in a smooth surface. This is an adaptation of the traditional Greek bag

GREEK BAG

Plain Weave with Laid-in Technique

The laid-in or brocading technique permits us to 'paint' with an additional weft thread in order to create varied pattern and colour effects on a plain weave background. A great favourite of weavers in Europe, Mexico and Central America, this technique is responsible for the beautiful peasant work that often resembles embroidery.

Although this bag is used as a carry-all, it can be a decorative hanging or a cushion cover as well. The technique is well suited to being used for blanket trims, scarves and table linens.

One common laid-in method is the 'straight laid-in', as in the gold bag. Here the pattern weft yarn is placed in the same sheds as the background plain weave. It weaves back and forth over only the area prescribed by the design, while the background weft travels from selvedge to selvedge.

For the laid-in method, the beginner should choose a simple or geometric design, such as is illustrated here. The design can be drawn, full-size, on plain paper and placed as a guide behind the weaving; or on graph paper with each square equal to the number of warp and weft threads determined by technique and yarns used.

Back of gold bag

The colour of the pattern thread should be in contrast to the background colour so it does not blend in and become lost. Since the weft is not beaten down to cover the warp, the colour of the warp must be considered as part of the background colour.

This technique can be woven with either the right side or the wrong side towards the weaver. I prefer weaving on the right side, but care must be taken at the point where the pattern thread turns so that turns are uniformly and neatly accomplished.

Another adaptation of the Greek bag. The braid forming the handle continues across the bottom of the bag

MATERIALS NEEDED – GOLD BAG

Warp 8/4 cotton, or linen or wool in a comparable weight, prepared for warp use. Black was used for the gold bag to tone down the brilliancy of colour. The warp can be in the same colour family as the weft or a complement or accent colour. Approximately 240 m (250 yds) are needed – about 170 gm (6 oz).

Weft and pattern All yarn used was lighter-weight linen yarn.

114 gm (4 oz) dull olive   57 gm (2 oz) lemon yellow
57 gm (2 oz) gold   114 gm (4 oz) dark gold
114 gm (4 oz) orange

CALCULATIONS

Sett 4 ends per cm (10 per in.). Double last two ends on each side for selvedge. Total number of ends, 124.
Width on loom 30 cm (12 in.).
Length For *frame loom*, a continuous warp; for *table or floor loom*, 1 m (approx 1 yd) plus loom allowance.

NOTE Each side of the bag is approximately 30 cm (12 in.) wide and 30 cm long, with a 2·5-cm (1-in.) allowance to turn back for the hem at the top opening of the bag. The back and the front are woven as a continuous piece.

Warp plan Straight draft (see page 47).
Tie up For plain weave.

STEPS IN CONSTRUCTION AND TECHNIQUE

Arrowhead pattern – straight laid-in Insert the pattern thread in the successive plain weave sheds either before *or* after the background weft and keep consistent throughout pattern. The turns are accomplished on the face of the cloth. Be careful when doing this to keep the turns even so that no unsightly loops are left on the surface.

Block pattern In the block design for the back of bag, the turns of the pattern weft are accomplished on the wrong side so that the surface of the fabric is smooth and without texture.

Prepare butterflies of your pattern colour. Use individual butterflies for each pattern section. Also have your drawing ready. I had each square of the graph

Arrowhead pattern. 'Straight laid-in' shows the turns on the face of the fabric

Block pattern. 'Straight laid-in' shows the turns on the wrong side of the fabric

equal two warp ends and one weft pick. Dull olive is the background colour for the back of the bag.

1. Weave in heading.
2. Start with back hem. Weave 2·5 cm (1 in.) dark gold.
3. Weave 2 cm ($\frac{3}{4}$ in.) orange band.
4. ·65 cm ($\frac{1}{4}$ in.) dull olive band.
5. 9·5 mm ($\frac{3}{8}$ in.) orange band.

6. 2 cm ($\frac{3}{4}$ in.) two orange blocks of laid-in. Open next shed, put in background weft. Beat down. With shed still open, count over to warp end where pattern begins, insert pattern butterfly from back of shed into open shed. Travel from right to left edge of pattern, bring butterfly out at back of shed. Beginning tail of butterfly can be turned around warp end at right edge of pattern. Do this for both orange blocks. Beat down, change sheds, put background in new shed. Beat,

insert weft butterfly from back, travelling left to right. Bring out of shed at rear, beat down. Continue in this manner until block is complete. Cut pattern thread, loop around warp end at end of pattern.

7. 18 mm (¾ in.) lemon yellow blocks — laid-in
8. 31·5 mm (1¼ in.) orange blocks — laid-in
9. 12·5 (½ in.) orange band
10. 9·5 mm (⅜ in.) gold band
11. 9·5 mm dull olive band
12. 6 mm (¼ in.) gold band
13. 6 mm lemon yellow band
14. 3 mm (⅛ in.) gold band
15. 9·5 mm dull olive band
16. 3 mm gold band
17. 9·5 mm orange band
18. 22 mm (1 in.) lemon yellow blocks — laid-in
19. 22 mm orange blocks — laid-in
20. 19 mm lemon yellow blocks — laid-in
21. 31·5 mm orange blocks — laid-in
22. 19 mm orange band
23. 9·5 mm gold band
24. 12·5 mm dull olive band — begins front of bag.
25. arrowhead and rosette motifs start here. 38 mm dull olive triangles — laid-in

Background colour is dark gold. Do laid-in as in step No 6, except always bring pattern butterflies to top surface at pattern edge and insert from top so that a small 'bump' appears where turn is made. Beginning and end of pattern thread are tucked in towards back of weaving.

26. 22 mm gold rosettes — laid-in
27. 16 mm (⅝ in.) orange squares — laid-in
28. 2 rows of 22 mm lemon yellow triangles — laid-in
29. 9·5 mm orange rosettes — laid-in
30. 22 mm gold triangles — laid-in
31. 22 mm lemon yellow triangles and 9·5 mm orange dots (turn on the inside) — laid-in
32. 22 mm dull olive triangles — laid-in
33. 12·5 mm 3 rows of orange laid-in, skip a shed in between so that laid-in always falls in same shed
34. 12·5 mm orange band
35. 12·5 mm same as step No 33
36. 38 mm (1½ in.) dull olive triangles — laid-in
37. 22 mm dark gold hem

FINISHING

1. Cut warp off loom, leaving warp ends about 5 to 7·5 cm (2 to 3 in.) long that can be tied, two together, or braided back so warp won't unravel.
2. If you want to line the bag, choose a medium-weight cotton twill, cut to size of bag less 5 cm (2 in.)
3. Seam up sides of bag and lining. Insert lining. Catch stitch lining top to bag. Turn hem in, catch stitch to lining. If lining is omitted, catch stitch hem to bag.
4. To make the carrying braid: cut two lengths each of two colours to make four lengths, each 4 m (160 in.) long. Fold lengths in half and put around a chair post so they will be taut while being braided.

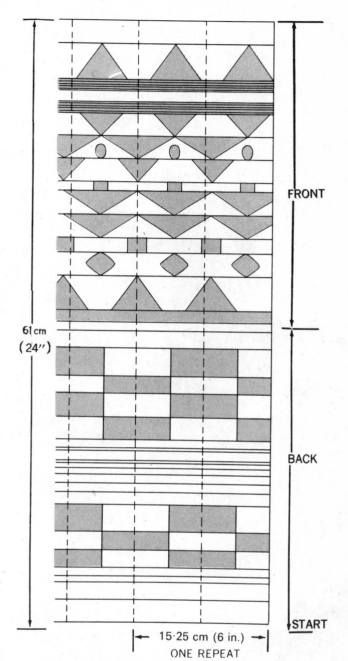

61 cm (24″)

15·25 cm (6 in.) ONE REPEAT

FRONT

BACK

START

Greek bag pattern. Start Step 2 at bottom of diagram and work up. Two repeats are needed to obtain width of the bag. Shaded areas indicate laid-in pattern

5. Adjust to proper length, sew to bag. Tassels, 10 cm (4 in.) long, can be added at corners or smaller ones across entire bottom of bag. If no tassels are used, the braid may be continued across bottom of bag.

HOW TO MAKE A FOUR STRAND BRAID

The design of this tapestry was suggested by a beach scene and woven in various tapestry techniques. Shells and novelty yarns create the texture

Other examples of handwoven fabrics are the Mexican plain weave upholstery and a window blind of mixed fibres and bamboo

TAPESTRY TECHNIQUE

A tapestry can be pure ornamentation as in a wall hanging, but the techniques are also used to weave handbags, belts, bands, rugs, and covers for footstools and small cushions. The basic weave is the same as that used in the background of the rya rug – plain weave beaten down over a widely spaced warp, covering it so that only the weft yarn shows. Since tapestries are usually representational or abstract patterns, they cannot be woven selvedge to selvedge on the same pick, but in sections according to how design motifs and colour fall. There are various techniques that provide for the joining of these sections or for a smooth transition from one section to another. As you will see, these techniques can also be used as design elements in the overall composition.

Before starting the tapestry it is essential to have a sketch of the design, known as a cartoon. Beginners should use a simple pattern. Keep the tapestry cartoon near at hand for easy checking – if convenient, attach it to the back of the warp. You could also paint the outlines of the design directly onto the warp. Working with simple areas gives you a chance to develop yarn and colour effects.

Tapestry weaving is usually done with the face away from the weaver; however, it can be woven face up if in this way the weaver feels more control over the desired effect.

The loom used can be of either the shaft or frame variety, although a true tapestry loom is more closely related to the frame loom.

Colour and design are taken care of by the weft. This can be almost any yarn – from the finest silk to the heaviest roving, from the shiniest flat metallic to the dullest texture. The warp is chosen for strength since the heavy beating down of the weft puts much stress on it. Linen, hard-twist wool, and cotton (sett at 3 to 5 ends per cm (8 to 12 per in.) are the yarns most frequently used.

Although it is fascinating to use many varied yarns and colours in a tapestry, results just as interesting can be achieved by a creative blending of a few carefully selected yarns and colours. The change from

This tapestry design was influenced by the landscape of a Greek island, Santorini. Several tapestry techniques were used to achieve the textural effects, seen in detail below one type of yarn to another within the tapestry should not be too rapid or an unnatural buckling in the surface will develop. Sometimes this can be steamed out at the finishing, but it is unwise to depend on this.

Since tapestry should ideally be a personal statement by the weaver, the project offered here is a sampler warp on which to try out the techniques that follow.

TECHNIQUES

1. Slit Vertical opening where two areas come together. When the weft threads of both areas reach their boundaries, they turn on adjacent warp threads and reverse direction. The slit that results may be left open – in some cases to form part of the design – or sewn together. Sewing is done when the tapestry is completed and on the wrong side with no stitches visible on the right side. Strong fine thread is run through the loops at the slit, going from one side of the slit to the other and drawing the edges together. When making a turn in the weaving, do not pull tightly on the weft or else the warp end, around which the turn is being made, will be pulled out of line, leaving a gap.

2. Dovetailing Vertical joining of weft threads, one from the right and one from the left, both turning around the same warp thread. This type of interlocking closes the space between sections and gives a vertical toothed pattern to the surface. The usual pattern of interlocking is 1 thread from each direction, but you could also use 2, 3 or 4 threads from each direction. Keep the number uniform in each section or an uneven effect will develop. The weaving must proceed at the same level or the joining will be askew. A slight ridge is made in the fabric at the point of dovetailing.

3. Interlocking Vertical joining of the weft threads from each direction by interlocking them between the warp ends before the weft threads reverse direction. Care must be taken that both weft threads are weaving in a straight line with each other and that a loose loop is not left at the point of interlocking.

4. Diagonal Natural closing in a tapestry formed by diminishing the area of one colour by a specified number of warp ends, and advancing the area of another colour. This progression moves over one warp end with each pick – or more, depending on how steep the pitch of the diagonal will be. Vertical slits will form if the pitch is very steep.

SUGGESTED PROJECT

Below is a diagram for a sampler warp. The numbers correspond to the techniques described. The areas are left unshaded. Copy the drawing below, then colour the areas as you wish.

(1) SLIT   **(2A)** DOVETAILING   **(2B)** DOVETAILING   **(3)** INTERLOCKING   **(4)** DIAGONAL

Warp Linen or cotton warp yarn. Linen should be at least a 5 ply with a hard twist. Cotton can be 8/4's. All yarns designated as 'rug warp' can be used.

Weft Experiment with yarns of different colours, weights and textures. Besides showing you the interesting effects you could plan into your tapestry, this experimenting will teach you where to make adjustments when using different weights of yarn so that the tapestry will lie smooth.

CALCULATIONS

Sett 3 to 4 ends per cm (8 to 10 per in.)
Width on loom 20 cm (8 in.).
Length $\frac{1}{2}$ m ($\frac{1}{2}$ yd) plus loom allowance.
Continuous warp on the frame loom.

DESIGN

The first 20 cm (8 in.) of the sampler are diagrammed here. But, since you will have enough warp on your loom, you can repeat this diagram in different colours and yarns until you have woven the techniques to your satisfaction – or you can change the diagram. You may want to practise one technique more than another, or change the angle of the design in some areas. Also you may want to incorporate shapes, ideas and techniques you have seen in other tapestries. These changes will increase your familiarity with the techniques and will make you aware of what shapes and effects are best in a tapestry. This is the first step in creating your own tapestry.

HELPFUL HINTS

1. Weave 2·5 to 5 cm (1 to 2 in.) plain weave headings at the beginning and end of your tapestry – rather loosely beaten in. These can be hemmed back later or taken out and a short fringe made.
2. A tapestry beater or ordinary household fork can be used to do the beating in individual sections. In some cases your fingers can help comb down the weft. Beating starts at point where weft entered shed and ends at point where weft exited. The weft should be in loosely enough to cover the warp without leaving loops on the surface after beating.

3. The weft is usually carried on small bobbins, specially made for tapestry weaving. The Gobelin bobbin and the Aubusson bobbin (called a flute) are shown here. The point of the Gobelin bobbin is used for beating down. I also use the butterflies and bobbins used for Argyle sock knitting.

GOBELIN BOBBIN

AUBUSSON FLUTE

4. Never carry threads over areas – cut and begin anew. To begin and end sections, put tail of weft thread around warp end at boundary and back into section under a couple of warp ends in same shed. All tails should be on the wrong side and can be clipped close at completion of tapestry. In cases where a bulky yarn does not permit this re-entering tails should be brought to the wrong side and darned in when the tapestry is off the loom.
5. Unless this is part of your design, selvedges and width of tapestry should be uniform throughout. Because of various weights and fibre contents involved in weft yarns and the weaving of shapes that distort the warp, a beginner may find the tapestry narrowing. To overcome this, darn a strong cord through both selvedges at intervals of 5 to 13 cm (2 to 5 in.). Stretch the tapestry to its intended width by pulling tightly on the cords. Tie the cords to both sides of the loom.

FINISHING

1. Machine stitch through the end rows of hem, unless you intend to make a fringe. The hem can be sewn to the tapestry with the sides left open so that dowels can be inserted and the tapestry hung.
2. Block before hemming. Attach the tapestry to a soft plywood board using non-rusting tacks or nails. Stretch it to the correct size, with corners square and edges even. Wet tapestry with warm water and let it dry thoroughly before removing tacks.
3. Alternately, wet a terry towel in warm water, wring out and place over section to be steamed. With a very hot iron, barely touch the towel. The full weight of the iron will not force as much steam through the tapestry and will only flatten the yarn. Allow the damp tapestry to dry slowly and thoroughly.

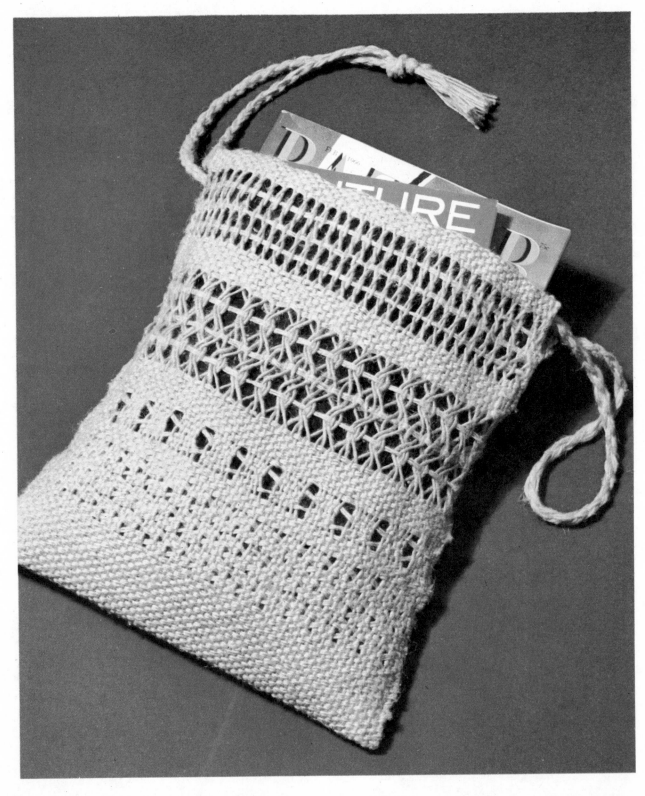

(*Above*) Purse with braided drawstring. Woven of thick linen roving in leno, double Mexican lace, and Spanish lace techniques. A lining of contrasting colour is added

(*Opposite*) Fine yarns may also be used in lace weaves, as in place mat at right. (Note that the place mat is woven in the lace technique only in specified areas)

LACE WEAVES

Leno, Mexican, Spanish

Up to now we have concentrated on a heavy beat and a covered, or nearly covered, warp. Now to the opposite effect – an open structure achieved by various techniques all under the heading of 'lace weaves'. Three of these techniques – leno, Spanish lace and Mexican lace – are used in the purses shown.

To create the open quality of lace, warp ends are pulled together by the weft or are twisted over each other. The warp must be strong to undergo the extra tension caused by the twisting. Since the twisted ends produce so much interest, it is better to keep the weft a solid colour, one close to the warp colour.

The different lace weaves can be used to decorate curtains or dress fabrics, table linens, cushion covers and shawls, or, on a large scale, screens or room divider panels.

SUGGESTED MATERIALS FOR PURSES

Warp Linen roving, 225 gms ($\frac{1}{2}$ lb) per purse.
Filling Linen roving, 115 gms ($\frac{1}{4}$ lb) per purse.
For a different shade or texture, try white wrapping twine (24 ply) or a finer weight linen, using two or three strands together.

CALCULATIONS

Sett 2 ends per cm (5 per in.) No 10 reed sleyed every other dent. Selvedges are not doubled in dent, but placed in adjoining dents. Only one extra thread on either side for selvedge. Total number of ends, 62.
Width on loom 30 cm (12 in.).
Length For *frame loom*, a continuous warp; for *table or floor model*, 1 m (1 yd) plus loom allowance. The first 25 to 30 cm (10 to 12 in.) can be used for practice. On the frame loom, a narrow practice warp is recommended before putting on the purse warp.
Length of purse No 1 Per side, 30 cm (12 in.) +2·5 cm (1 in.) hem.
Length of purse No 2 Per side, 30 cm+2·5 cm hem.
Warp plan Straight draft (see page 47).

TECHNIQUES

Leno

Leno is the most common lace weave and structurally the simplest. With a pick-up stick (see Glossary), pull the warp ends from the lower layer of the shed to the right, up and over an equal number of warp ends in the top layer. Leno is always worked from right to left for the first twist.

Leno weaves as worked from selvedge to selvedge (*left*). The ends are twisted to create open spaces, as worked in sections (*right*). Plain weave is built up around sections so that weaving proceeds evenly across the web

In the following directions one end from the lower layer is twisted over one in the top layer and worked across the entire web, as in the purses. Or, two or three ends can be twisted together using an equal number in both layers of the shed. Leno can also be woven in blocks, separated by sections of plain weave. Before you do these variations, put your pattern on graph paper. Each square should equal a given number of warp ends and weft picks, according to thickness of yarn and number of ends involved in a twist.

1. Plain weave, ending with a left to right shot of weft.
2. Beat in last pick of plain weave, change shed. Beat again, leave shed open. Put weft thread aside and take pick-up stick.
3. Start from right side, put the flat side of the stick under first end in lower shed. Lift end, move with it on stick to right of first upper end.
4. Slide stick with lower end on it over first upper end (this is the actual twist) and down under second lower end.
5. Pick up second lower end on stick, bring to right, up and over second upper end.

6. Move stick down to third lower end and continue in above manner.
7. When you finish the row, all the ends from the lower shed should be on the stick. Close shed, turn pick-up stick on its edge to form a new shed. Insert weft right to left. Return stick to level position to close shed.
8. With stick push down new weft as far as it will go, but don't force it. Remove stick. The twist has been locked into position by the weft.
9. Beat down again. Check that spaces formed by the twist are even all the way across.
10. Open plain weave shed, insert weft left to right. This gives an automatic twist to the ends. Continue steps 2 to 9 for more leno or return to plain weave.

Mexican Lace

This is a more elaborate form of leno. The twist here is also between the upper and lower layers of the shed, but the twisting order is uneven. This difference adds more curve to the warp ends, but it also adds more stress. Therefore, care should be exercised in beating or the ends may snap.

There is single Mexican lace and double Mexican lace – so called according to the number of ends twisted together.

Single Mexican lace (*left*) worked across web. Note that the curve in the twist is greater here than in leno. Three rows of double Mexican lace (*right*)

1. Plain weave on last pick from left to right.
2. Single twist – one end twisted over another except at selvedge. With pick-up stick go under the two

lower warp ends on right. Pull towards right of first upper end. Go over upper end, dip under next one in lower warp (end No 3). Pick this up on stick also. Go over the next end at right in upper warp.

3. Continue picking up one under, move to right, over one upper.

4. At selvedge, one lower end goes over two upper ends. Close shed.

5. Stand stick on end, put weft through new shed, right to left.

6. Level pick-up stick and push weft down with it.

7. Beat down again with comb and beater, making sure that twist is even all the way across.

8. Change shed, put plain weave through left to right which automatically gives a second twist. Continue with Mexican lace or plain weave.

9. Double twist – two lower ends twisted over two upper ends. Follow above directions but begin at the right selvedge by pulling three lower ends to the right and over two upper ends. Go under next two in lower shed. Pull to right, go up and over two upper ends. Continue to selvedge where two lower ends go over three upper ends. Close shed.

10. Stand stick on end, insert weft in new shed right to left. Level stick, push down weft.

11. Change shed, beat again, put weft through left to right. Continue with Mexican lace or plain weave.

Spanish Lace

A subtler pattern than leno or Mexican, it is made by weaving over a fixed number of warp ends, then pulling them together into a group. This number is fixed by the size and shape of the pattern desired and the type of yarn used. The width of the opening between the groups is determined by how tightly the weft yarn

Spanish lace, worked in sections of ten ends

Diagram showing how to divide groups of ends for a staggered effect in Spanish lace

is pulled back. However, you may choose not to pull the groups together in order to keep the small pattern that develops between them. The pattern can also be changed by altering the direction of the weaving. These pattern variations become more pronounced if the weft thread is much thicker and softer than the warp thread. The directions given are for four-end Spanish lace.

NOTE The weft yarn should be in butterflies for easier manipulation between the small groups of warp ends. A pick-up stick is not used in making Spanish lace.

1. Plain weave on last pick, left to right.

2. Open next shed, pass weft through right to left under half the number of ends in your pattern. Thus, if your pattern group is four ends, as here, then two ends would be in each shed.

3. Bring weft to surface. Beat down with comb. The beater on a table or floor loom is not usually used for this weave.

4. Change sheds, insert weft left to right under the two warp ends. Pull the ends gently but firmly into a tight group. Beat down.

5. Change shed, insert weft right to left. Go under the two ends in first group *and also* two of the next group. Pull the first group together as you bring weft to surface. Beat down.

6. Change sheds, insert weft left to right under the two ends in the group No 2 and come to the surface. Pull this group together and beat down.

7. Change sheds, insert weft right to left going under the two ends of group No 2 and two ends of group No 3. Pull group No 2 together, beat down. As can be seen, you weave right, left, and right in one group before proceeding to the next group.

8. Change sheds, continue in this manner.

9. After finishing a row, return to the right selvedge *via* plain weave, or weave the same pattern but count over left to right. In this case weave left, right, and left before moving to the next group.

STEPS IN CONSTRUCTION

Combined here are the three lace weaves and the plain weave. The areas where they are used, plus their lengths in centimetres, are based on using linen roving in warp and weft.

Bamboo Handle Purse

1. 38 mm (1½ in.) plain weave – includes hem
2. 86 mm (3⅜ in.) double Mexican lace –
   3 rows of twists
   4 rows of spaces
3. 16 mm (⅝ in.) plain weave
4. 28·5 mm (1⅛ in.) – 1 row of single Mexican lace
5. 16 mm plain weave
6. 51 mm (2 in.) – leno –
   3 rows of twists
   4 rows of spaces
7. 16 mm plain weave
8. 28·5 mm – 1 row of single Mexican lace
9. 51 mm plain weave

This completes one side of the purse. To weave the other side, reverse directions No 9 through No 1.

Drawstring Purse

1. 57 mm (2¼ in.) plain weave, includes hem
2. 51 mm leno, 3 rows twists, 4 rows of spaces
3. 255 mm (1 in.) plain weave
4. 86 mm double Mexican lace, 3 rows of twists
   4 rows of spaces
5. 25·5 mm plain weave
6. 25·5 mm Spanish lace, 6 ends in group, weave 1st row, left to right
   weave 2nd row, right to left
7. 12·5 mm (½ in.) plain weave
8. 54 mm (2⅛ in.) Spanish lace, 4 ends in group, stagger each group
9. 57 mm plain weave

This completes one side of the purse. To weave the other side, reverse directions, from No 9 to No 1.

Casement cloth, of linen roving and wrapping twine, using three techniques – the bottom section in Spanish lace, the middle Mexican lace, the top leno

HELPFUL HINTS

1. The extra tension added to the warp ends during the twisting or pulling must be lessened or the warp ends will break. On the floor or table loom release the back ratchet as soon as you feel the warp tightening too much. On the frame loom, insert additional tension sticks to top and bottom of loom as the warp is wound around it. Then when you make the lace weave, these sticks can be removed to lessen tension and then reinserted, if necessary, for plain weave.

2. You must start the lace technique with the first selvedge thread on the right in the upper shed if you are working from selvedge to selvedge.

3. Have the weft in butterflies, on stick shuttles, or on very small boat shuttles in order to get it easily through the picked-up shed.

4. In working from selvedge to selvedge, be sure the weft is not pulled in too tightly. Lace areas tend to draw in, but are also somewhat elastic and will steam and block out to the required width.

5. To beat down, use pick-up stick, comb or, in some cases, the beater. Spanish lace is easily pushed down with the fingers or a very narrow pick-up stick.

6. A white paper placed behind the warp will help you see the ends better.

7. Count, to be sure you have the correct number of ends on pick-up stick.

FINISHING

1. Overhand stitch at beginning and end of purse before removing warp from loom.

2. Block and press with steam iron for even selvedges.

3. Cut lining to size of purse, less hem. Slip stitch to purse.

4. Fold hem of plain weave over lining. Catch stitch to lining.

5. For purse with drawstring, seam up sides only to the hem so that the drawstring can be inserted at the side into the casing formed by the hem. Make a braid 2 m (80 in.) long, as shown on page 69, to pull through hem casing. Tie ends of drawstring together after pulling through.

6. For purse with bamboo handle, seam up sides and attach wooden or bamboo handle.

Purse with bamboo handles, woven of linen roving in the Mexican lace and leno techniques

STOLE, CUSHION COVERS

Simple Weaves for the 4- Shaft Loom

In the preceding pages you learned how simple techniques can lead to beautiful items of practical or aesthetic value. There is still much more that could be experimented with on a frame loom or using two sheds on a shaft loom. Eventually, however, you will want to do some weaving on a larger loom that offers more structural and design possibilities. Therefore, the remaining pages are devoted to projects that will initiate you into weaving on a 4-shaft loom.

I strongly recommend that the first item you weave on the 4-shaft loom is a sample warp based on the weaves mentioned on page 45. This will acquaint you with the relationship between weave draft, drawing-in draft, and tie-up of treadles and order of treadling – or, as on a table loom, the order of pushing down the levers. The lifting plans are for the rising shed loom.

Following are directions for three small projects. They include cushion covers and a stole. The weave draft is not illustrated. The warp plan, or drawing-in draft, is a straight draft in all cases. The lifting plan with instructions for both table and floor loom, is indicated by each project. Although the 4-shaft loom was used in all cases, the drafts can be adapted for looms with more shafts.

Cushion cover woven in a combination of twill and plain weaves with a multicoloured weft of textured yarns

Small cushion cover of red and gold yarns, woven in plain weave on a 4-shaft loom. Gold metallic thread is used to highlight the centre bands

Lightweight stole with fringe, in a twill weave. Note the off-centre stripe in the warp

LIGHTWEIGHT STOLE

Stripe Pattern in Warp

Suggested materials for 2-m (72-in.) stole. 2/17's weaving worsted. Turquoise – 225 gm ($\frac{1}{2}$ lb) – for both warp and weft; 56 gm (2 oz) black, for warp only.

Sett 8 ends per cm (20 per in.) – No 40–10 reed sleyed 2 per dent. Total number of ends, 400+8 for selvedge (4 on each side).

Width in reed 50 cm (20 in.).

Length of warp 2 m (2 yds)+loom allowance.

Warping order 50 T, 12 B, 10 T, 48 B, 15 T, 15 B, 8 T, 6 B, 244 T.

KEY T = Turquoise B = Black

Warp plan Straight draw, single in heddles.

Weft Solid turquoise used singly.

Weave $\frac{2}{2}$ twill. Treadles are tied up to shafts indicated. Treadle order is 1–4 repeated for the entire stole.

Finishing Cut off loom. Fray out a 10-cm (3$\frac{1}{2}$-in.) fringe at each end. Separate fringe into small groups of about 15 to 20 ends and knot close to woven fabric so picks are secured in place. Wash in mild soap and warm water.

LIFTING PLAN FOR LIGHTWEIGHT STOLE

Detail of stole showing twill weave

SMALL CUSHION COVER

Bands of Pattern in Contrasting Colour Yarn and Metallic Yarn

Suggested materials 2/20's weaving worsted. Completed size is 40×40 cm (15×15 in.). 114 gm (4 oz) gold and 114 gm (4 oz) red for both warp and weft; 28 gm (1 oz) gold metallic giumpe yarn, for weft only.

Sett 6 ends per cm (15 per in.), No 60–10 reed sleyed 1 per dent. Total number of ends, 255+4 for selvedge (2 on each side).

Width in reed 44 cm (17 in.).

Length of warp 1 m (1 yd)+loom allowance.

Warping order 1 gold, 1 red.

Warp plan Straight draft, single in heddles.

Weft Back of cushion is solid red. Front is a pattern of wide bands, randomly arranged in gold and red and alternating with 9·5-mm ($\frac{3}{8}$-in.) wide bands of solid red weft. The arrangement of the predominantly gold bands is as follows, after 44 cm (17 in.) of solid red weft.

BAND NO 1	BAND NO 2	BAND NO 4	BAND NO 6
2 G ⎫ × 2	2 G	2 G + M ⎫	2 G
2 R ⎭	2 R	2 R ⎬ × 2	2 R
2 R	3 G	1 G + M ⎭	1 G
3 G	1 R ⎫ × 2	1 G + M	4 R
2 R	1 G ⎭	3 R	1 G ⎫ × 2
1 G	1 G	2 G + M	2 R ⎭
	1 R	2 R ⎬ × 3	2 G
	2 R ⎫ × 2	3 G + M	2 R
	2 G ⎭	1 G + M ⎫ × 2	1 G
		3 R ⎭	3 R
		3 G + M	4 G
		1 R	1 R
			1 G

(KEY: R = red, G = gold, M = metallic, X = times)

Band No 3 Like band No 1 but with metallic thread added in with every gold pick.

Band No 5 Like band No 2 but with metallic thread added in with every gold pick.

Band No 7 Like band No 6 minus last 2 picks and reading column from bottom to top.

Band No 8 Like band No 6 minus last 2 picks and first 2 picks.

Band No 9 Like band No 6 minus last 6 picks.
Weave Plain weave beaten down fairly heavy.
Lifting plan See page 48 for plain weave on a 4-shaft loom.
Finishing Cut off loom. Run a line of machine stitching at both cut ends of cloth to keep weft from fraying. Wash in soap and warm water. Fit to cushion size and seam two selvedge sides on wrong side of cloth. Invert and insert cushion. Sew opening.

MULTICOLOURED CUSHION

Bands of Textured Yarn

Suggested materials 2-ply wool (suiting weight), Nordic rya yarn, knitting worsted, wool *bouclé* (or any heavy textured yarn). Amounts given are for finished cushion size 48 × 36 cm (19 × 14 in.). Reddish-purple, brown, wine, red (2-ply wool) – 57 gm (2 oz) of each for warp.
Brilliant purple Nordic rya yarn – 115 gm (4 oz) for weft.
Royal blue knitting worsted – 57 gm (2 oz) for weft.
Deep turquoise wool *bouclé* – 57 gm (2 oz) for weft.
Sett 8 ends per cm (20 per in.) – No 40–10 reed sleyed 2 per dent. Total number of ends, 400+4 for selvedge (2 on each side).
Width in reed 50 cm (20 in.).
Length of Warp 1 m (1 yd) +loom allowance.
Warping order 1 red, 1 brown, 1 purple, 1 wine.
Warp plan Straight draft, 2 ends in each heddle.
Weft Back and front of cushion cover are the same. After doing one side, start the second side with 25·5 mm (1 in.) (1B, 1T) and end with 51 mm (2 in.) P.

LIFTING PLAN FOR MULTICOLOURED CUSHION

TREADLE NO

SHAFT NO   4 3 2 1

LEVERS ON
TABLE LOOM

NOTE. The A and B designations in the lifting plan always denote the plain weave tie-up of the treadles

Weave Plain weave in purple sections and in blue and purple sections; broken twill in the turquoise and blue sections and the solid blue in these areas.

Treadles A and B are tied up for plain weave. 1, 4, 2, 3, for a $\frac{2}{2}$ broken twill. Follow both weaves in consecutive order, but mix weaves together when colour calls for it.
Finishing Follow directions as given for red and gold cushion cover.

(**KEY:** B = blue, T = turquoise, P = purple, X = times) Where inches are not indicated, measurement is in picks.

COL 1	COL 2
12·5 mm (½ in.) P	12·5 mm (½ in.) P
25·5 mm (1 in.)	2 B
(1 B, 1 T)	
25·5 mm (1 in.) P	1 P ⎫ × 2
1 B ⎫ × 2	1 B ⎭
1 T ⎭	1 T
2 B	1 B
12·5 mm (½ in.) P	12·5 mm (½ in.) P
1 B ⎫ × 4	1 B ⎫ × 3
1 T ⎭	1 T ⎭
5 B	5 B
1 B ⎫ × 3	1 B ⎫ × 2
1 T ⎭	1 T ⎭
8 B	3 B
1 B ⎫ × 3	12·5 mm (½ in.) P
1 T ⎭	4 B
	2 P

COL 3	COL 4
1 B ⎫ × 4	2 B
1 T ⎭	1 B ⎫ × 4
1 B	1 T ⎭
2 P	4 B
1 B ⎫ × 2	1 B ⎫ × 3
1 T ⎭	1 T ⎭
7 B	1 B
1 B ⎫ × 3	12·5 mm (½ in.) P
1 T ⎭	2 B
1 B	3 P
12·5 mm (½ in.) P	1 B ⎫ × 2
2 B	1 T ⎭
2 P	1 B
1 B ⎫ × 2	38 mm (1½ in.) P
1 T ⎭	

Poncho of medium-weight wool with braided tie at neckline. A very popular garment from South America, this is a straight piece of weaving and requires no sewing

DRESS FABRICS

Wider Fabrics Using Variations on Weaves

After you have become accustomed to weaving on a loom more complex than the frame variety, you will undoubtedly begin to think of weaving larger projects and will want to try out variations on the simple weave structures we have used thus far. Fabrics that seem to fall into this class are those woven as yardage for suits, skirts, dresses and coats.

Simple weaves are very well suited to dress fabrics and do not conflict with the colour arrangement nor do they overshadow the textured yarns that enhance many of these fabrics. The 'homespun look' of much of our commercially produced sport and casual fabrics is in reality our old friend, the plain weave. Another popular weave found in dress fabrics is the twill weave which produces a cloth that is elegant, drapes well and has a lustrous surface.

Tweed coat-dress of woollen fabric in a plain weave

Weaving tweeds is a natural for the handloom. These tweeds can be almost any combination from related hues subtly arranged as in the poncho to an effect as bold as the 'salt and pepper' in the coat dress.

In the projects given here, I obtained the colour effect I wanted by using two threads as one in the warp. In these instances the warp is threaded double in the heddles.

As before, a small sample warp is suggested so that you can see the result before investing in yarns for the yardage. Also ideas may develop that did not occur to you originally.

Detail of poncho showing weave and colour arrangement. Warp and weft threads are used double for weight and colour effect

Lightweight yarns are best for suiting and dresses; the heavier ones should be saved for coating. The picks per centimetre should be the same as the ends per centimetre, or less. In finishing, the cloth will shrink sufficiently to give a fabric that is firm but pliable enough to sew.

For weavers not handy with a needle, there are woven garments that require little or no sewing. One such item is the poncho described here. This is an idea transported to us from South America and very popular with students and for country and leisure wear.

In weaving these wide fabrics be sure to throw your shuttle with enough force to send it to the other side of the loom; if not, it may fall through the warp shed to the bottom. Also take care not to pull the selvedges in too tightly since a looser selvedge shrinks in better. The beat should be even throughout the fabric so that streaks will not result from where picks have been suddenly placed in too loosely or too tightly.

MEDIUM-WEIGHT PONCHO WITH SUBTLE STRIPE EFFECT

Suggested materials 2-ply wool (suiting weight), 3-ply (medium-weight) rug wool, knitting worsted. **NOTE** The poncho was woven for a person of medium to tall height and falls slightly above the knee. Amounts given are for this size.

Reddish purple 335 gm ($\frac{3}{4}$ lb) (2-ply suiting wool) – warp

Brown 335 gm ($\frac{3}{4}$ lb) (2-ply suiting wool) – warp

Wine 450 gm (1 lb) (2-ply suiting wool) – warp and weft

Red 450 gm (1 lb) (2-ply suiting wool) – warp and weft

Rust 335 gm ($\frac{3}{4}$ lb) (3-ply medium-weight rug wool) – weft

Burnt orange 225 gm ($\frac{1}{2}$ lb) (knitting worsted) – weft

Magenta 335 gm ($\frac{3}{4}$ lb) (knitting worsted) – weft

Sett 8 ends per cm (20 per in.) – No 40–10 reed sleyed 2 per dent. Total number of ends, 900+8 for selvedge (4 on each side).
Width in reed 1·15 m (45 in.).
Length of warp 2·5 m (2½ yds) + loom allowance.
Warping order 1 red, 1 brown, 1 purple, 1 wine.
Warp plan Straight draft – 2 ends in each heddle.

Weft Wine, red, rust, burnt orange and magenta.

28 cm (11 in.) red and rust (used as 1 pick)—including 38 mm (1½ in.) hem

12·5 mm (½ in.) burnt orange (2 strands used as 1 pick)

19 mm (¾ in.) red and rust

9·5 mm (⅜ in.) burnt orange

9·5 mm (⅜ in.) red and rust

28·5 mm (1⅛ in.) burnt orange

16 mm (⅝ in.) red and rust

63·5 mm (2½ in.) magenta and wine (used as 1 pick)

9·5 mm (⅜ in.) red and rust

16 mm (⅝ in.) burnt orange

16 mm (⅝ in.) red and rust

9·5 mm (⅜ in.) burnt orange

22 mm (⅞ in.) red and rust

6 mm (¼ in.) burnt orange

10 cm (4 in.) red and rust

6 mm (¼ in.) burnt orange

9·5 mm (⅜ in.) red and rust

16 mm (⅝ in.) burnt orange

9·5 mm (⅜ in.) red and rust

29·2 cm (11½ in.) magenta and wine

This finishes one side of the poncho.

For the back side, continue until magenta and wine section measures 60 cm (23 in.) in all. Then proceed up the column back to the hem. The slit for the head begins at the start of the magenta and wine section and continues upwards for 38 cm (15 in.). To make the slit, find the centre of the warp and then work two shuttles simultaneously, one going from the right selvedge to the slit, and the other from the slit to the left selvedge. The slit opening should have an even edge. Do not pull at the edge threads with the weft or the slit will appear distorted.

Weave Broken twill in red and rust sections, plain weave in burnt orange and magenta sections.

Finishing Wash in mild soap and lukewarm water. Hem. For the tie, make a 3-strand braid of the

LIFTING PLAN FOR PONCHO

TREADLE NO

B	4	2		
A	3	1		
4	4	3		
3	4	1		
2	3	2		
1	2	1		

SHAFT NO   4 3 2 1

LEVERS ON TABLE LOOM

NOTE. The A and B designations in the lifting plan always denote the plain weave tie-up of the treadles various colours used in the warp. Knot the ends leaving a 5-cm (2-in.) fringe. Pull through cloth, 16·5 cm (6½ in.) up from the bottom of slit and on either side of slit, being careful not to break any ends or picks. If you do not wish to have braided tie, make the slit about 15·25 cm (6 in.) shorter.

TWEED FABRIC FOR A COAT-DRESS

Suggested materials 2/20's worsted, 2/17's worsted, 2-ply wool (suiting weight). French novelty wool yarn, cotton novelty slub yarn.

NOTE The coat-dress takes 4·5 m (4¾ yds) of 90-cm (35-in.) wide fabric for a size 14. Figure your yardages according to your correct size and the type of garment you wish to make. Use this finished length in your calculations to find the dressed length; be careful to allow for the take-up and, in the width, the draw-in.

1. ·225 kg (½ lb) light wine 2/20's worsted — warp
2. ·225 kg (½ lb) deep wine, 2/20's worsted — warp
3. ·115 kg (¼ lb) off-white 2/17's worsted — warp
4. ·225 kg (½ lb) black/white cotton novelty slub yarn — warp
5. ·225 kg (½ lb) black/white French novelty wool yarn — warp
6. 1·021 kg (2¼ lb) white/wine 2-ply wool (suiting weight) — warp and weft

Sett 8 ends per cm (20 per in.) — No 40–10 reed sleyed 2 per dent. Total number of ends, 816+8 for selvedge (4 on each side).

Width in reed 1 m 2 cm (40 in.).

Length of warp 4·6 m (5 yds) +loom allowance.

Warping order 1,5,6,4,3,2, repeat — refer to yarn list above.

Warp plan Straight draft, every third heddle has two ends in it.

Weft Solid white/wine 2-ply wool.

Weave Plain weave.

Lifting plan For plain weave – see page 48.

Finishing Machine-stitch beginning and end of yardage so picks will not fray out. Wash in mild soap and warm water. Let dry and steam press.

Detail of coat-dress fabric. The character of the plain weave is changed completely by the yarn combination in both warp and weft

UPHOLSTERY FABRICS

Heavier Fabrics Using Complex Warp Plan and Weaves

When a more complex warp plan is used, the opportunities for pattern and textural effects expand limitlessly.

Up to now we have been using the straight draft warp plan on the 4-shaft loom, but used here for the upholstery fabric is a variation of a warp plan for the weave commonly called 'honeycomb'. Instead of using the lifting plan usually associated with this weave, I tried variations until I got the fabrics I wanted for my dining-room chairs. By referring to the photographs shown, you can see the entirely different weaves obtained in the fabric. The lifting plans were based on plain weave and the warp-faced twill weave, but a combination weave resulted from the mixing of these two lifting plans.

The honeycomb warp plan tends to give long floats of weft on the reverse side. Because of this the fabric would not lend itself to uses that expose both sides nor to those where the floats could be easily caught or pulled. It lends itself perfectly, however, as a covering for a chair seat or footstool where the reverse side would not show. However, whenever the reverse side is exposed – as it would be in a purse, for example – a lining should be added.

When weaving upholstery, it is necessary to have strong yarns and a weave that will stand much wear. Also, construction must be tight so that the threads will not shift. A tight construction is one in which the sett is high, or dense, and the beat is heavy, making the number of picks per centimetre proportionately high. A tight construction is also necessary so that the padding of the chair seat, for example, will not show through as the fabric is being stretched to fit.

The five swatches shown here and on the opposite page are all upholstery fabrics made on the same warp. Their variations result from differences in weave structure and colour placement. The red swatch is in plain weave with a solid red weft. The other four are in combination weaves with mixed colours in the weft

Honeycomb ridged effect

Honeycomb textural effect

The honeycomb warp plan produces a heavy fabric that gives a subtle ridge effect caused by dips that travel the length of the warp, as shown on left; or a textural effect caused by small raised dots as shown on right

On the previous page is illustrated a fabric to be used as seat covers for chairs. The finished width is the width of the chair seats, plus the allowance needed for tucking under.

UPHOLSTERY FABRIC FOR DINING-ROOM CHAIRS

Suggested materials 3- or 4-ply rug wool. If lighter weight yarn is used, it should be set very dense in the reed, or two or three threads used as one. For the chair illustrated, a piece of fabric 71 × 58 cm (28 × 23 in.) is needed.

Royal blue	115 gm (4 oz) warp
Bright purple	115 gm (4 oz) warp
Deep teal (greenish-blue)	115 gm (4 oz) warp

WARP PLAN FOR HONEYCOMB WEAVE

SHAFT NO

Ridged Effect

Deep rose	115 gm (4 oz) weft yarn
Dull violet	115 gm (4 oz) weft yarn
Red	57 gm (2 oz) weft yarn

Sett 5 ends per cm (12 per in.). Total number of ends, 405+8 for selvedges (4 on each side).
Width in reed 81 cm (32 in.) wide.
Length of warp 58·4 cm (23 in.)+loom allowance.
Warping order 1 purple, 1 royal blue, 1 teal repeated throughout.
Warp plan Single in heddles.

Weft 2 dull violet, 1 deep rose, 1 red, 1 deep rose repeated throughout.
Lifting plan The order of treadling is: A, B, 1, 2, 1, repeat. The corresponding levers would be pushed on a table loom.

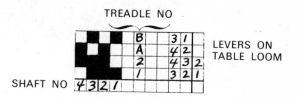

Finishing Machine stitch beginning and end of fabric. Wash in mild soap and luke-warm water.

Textural Effect

Teal	170 gm (6 oz) weft yarn
Brown	170 gm (6 oz) weft yarn

Sett Width in reed, total number of ends, length of warp, warping order, warp plan – as for Ridged Effect at left.

Weft 4 brown, 4 blue repeated throughout.
Lifting plan The order of treadling is: 1, 2, 1, 2, A, B, A, B, 3, 4, 3, 4, A, B, A, B, repeat. The corresponding levers would be pushed on a table loom.

Finishing As for Ridged Effect at left.

COLONIAL OVERSHOT

The pattern structure called 'colonial overshot' is an example of a weave that looks more complex than it actually is. You will eventually be able to analyse such fabrics and see with what simplicity and logic they have been constructed.

Called 'colonial overshot' because we associate it with our early settlers, this type of weaving is also known in Scandinavia, the Balkans and Greece – but it was not known in England until recently, so it is doubtful that it was brought to the USA by the Pilgrims. Even so, it remains a true heritage from the early founders of this country. It seems to have been an especially favoured product of our colonial weavers and examples of it, particularly in coverlets, are found in many museums and early American restorations.

The weave is in three colours – the pattern, the background, and the pattern and background combined.

The overshot forms the pattern; it skips over the ground weave and creates a pattern of short floats. The yarn used for the pattern should be soft, but heavier than the background weft so that it can be beaten down well and still stand out boldly. The background is formed by the warp and weft – usually of the same thread count. The third colour is formed by the pattern interweaving with the background.

The background is a plain weave. The pattern weave is based usually on twill blocks. That is 1,2 weave together, 2,3,3,4, and 4,1. The way in which the loom is threaded brings areas of these blocks together to form the pattern. Between every pick of pattern weft, there is one pick of plain weave. In the warp plan an odd number has to follow an even number since this way we can be sure that the plain weave will be constructed correctly.

The directions given are for the cushion cover, 50 × 30 cm (20 × 12 in.). If you wish to adapt this pattern for the coverlet, take the pattern motif marked on the warp plan and repeat it enough times to fulfil the width of your coverlet; then add the border pattern.

(*Above*) 'Monk's Belt', a simple adaptation of overshot, showing a section of reverse side. (*Below*) Detail of traditional coverlet in the Double Bowknot pattern, wool and cotton, woven in Ohio in 1867. (Courtesy The Smithsonian Institute)

On the same threading two pattern variations are possible. The cushion cover in the 'Lover's Knot' pattern (*above left*) and the bedspread (*opposite page*) were developed from the sample warps (*above right*).

'LOVER'S KNOT' CUSHION COVER

Suggested materials 15/3's mercerized cotton and 2/7's homespun wool.

Rose 15/3 cotton 170 gm (6 oz) warp and weft background.

Red 2/7 Nordic homespun pattern weft 170 gm (6 oz).

Sett 8 ends per cm (20 per in.). Total number of ends; 424+4 for selvedge (2 on each side).

Width in reed 53 cm (21 in.) reed.

Length of warp 26 in. +loom allowance.

Warping order Solid rose cotton.

Warp plan As illustrated in draft – single in heddles.

Weft Rose cotton on plain weave, red wool on pattern weave.

Hem Start with 25·5 mm (1 in.) plain weave. *Do not forget* that between every pick of pattern listed there is one of plain weave.

Treadling Order

BORDER	CENTRE MOTIF		SMALL MOTIF
*2–5x	4–3x	1–3x	
1–4x	3–3x	2–3x	1–3x
2–2x	2–3x	3–5x	2–3x
1–4x	1–3x	4–4x	1–3x
2–5x	2–2x	3–2x	
		†4–2x	

x = Times.

*Treadle No

†From here, work back to first motif pick to complete circle.

Repeat centre motif twice and border once to complete the front. The back may be all plain weave or the same pattern as front.

Finishing Seam three sides, right sides together. Invert and insert cushion. Sew top seam, making sure to fold hem under.

WARP PLAN

SELVEDGE

BORDER

REPEAT 3 TIMES FOR CUSHION

A continuous draft for the 'Lover's Knot' cushion

Glossary

Apron The canvas that attaches the apron bars to either the warp beam or cloth beam.

Apron bars Thin, strong, wood or metal rods to which the warp is attached at the front and back of the loom.

Back beam The stationary upper beam behind the loom directly over the warp beam. Helps to keep the warp at an even tension by giving it a smooth surface to glide over. Also called slabstock.

Beaming Winding the warp onto the warp beam under tension.

Beater The movable frame that holds the reed. Pulling it forwards pushes the weft into place in the warp. Also called batten.

Bobbin Weft thread is wound around this before it is inserted into the shuttle. Also called quill or spool.

Breast beam Stationary top beam at the front of the loom over which the woven cloth passes to the cloth beam below.

Butterfly A hand-bobbin arrangement of weft yarn, used without a holder and made by winding the yarn around the fingers in a figure of eight.

Castle See **Top castle.**

Chain A series of continuous loops (similar to a crochet chain) made in the warp to shorten its length temporarily; for easier handling from the warping device to the loom and to prevent tangling.

Chain draft See **Lifting plan.**

Chain spacer Crochet-like loops made around the warp ends in a frame loom before weaving begins, to keep warp ends evenly spaced.

Cloth beam The rotating lower front beam of loom on which the finished cloth is rolled as it is woven.

Counterbalanced loom A loom with a sinking shed. See **Sinking shed.**

Cross Formed as warp ends cross in alternate succession around pegs on a warping board or reel. It simplifies the threading of the loom by keeping the ends in order and free from tangles. Also called lease.

Dent The space between two bars in a reed. Reeds come in various sizes according to the number of dents per 10 cm they carry.

Draft A drawing of a weave pattern on graph paper showing its threading and weaving order.

Drawing-in Threading the warp ends through the heddle eyes and the reed dents.

Dressing the loom Preparing the loom for weaving.

Ends Individual lengths of warp threads.

Fibres Synthetic or natural hair-like filaments which when spun together form thread or yarn.

Filling See **Weft.**

Harness A complete set of shafts of heddles.

Heading A narrow band of heavy yarn, string or rags woven in at the beginning of the fabric.

Heddle Flat metal strip, string or wire with a loop or eye in its centre that is suspended between the shaft sticks. Holds the warp threads in position.

Heddle cords See **Leashes.**

Heddle eye Loop or opening in the centre of heddle through which the warp ends are threaded according to pattern chosen.

Heddle rod The bar that carries the looped cord heddles on frame, tapestry and stick looms.

Jack loom A loom with a rising shed. See **Rising Shed.**

Lams Horizontal levers between the shafts and treadles and attached to both.

Lease See **Cross.**

Lease rods Flat, thin, smooth sticks inserted into the warp on either side of the cross to keep the cross in order while beaming and threading the loom. Also called lease stick.

Leashes Long loops of cord attached to the heddle rod of a frame loom. The alternate warp ends pass through these to form one of the sheds.

Levers The bars on table looms which raise the shafts when pressed.

Lifting plan A plan that indicates which shafts to raise and in what order to raise them.

Loom A frame for holding the warp ends under tension so weaving can take place.

Mordants The chemical compounds used to set colour.

Pick A single passage of weft thread through the shed. Also called shot.

Pick-up stick A thin, flat, bevelled stick with a pointed end. Used as an aid in making extra shed openings for pattern weaving. 2·5 to 5 cm (1 to 2 in.) wide.

Piecing Starting a new thread where an old one has ended. Usually means the overlapping of the threads or rags used in the weft.

Pile The strands or loops of weft yarn that are so woven as to be raised above the surface of the cloth. Short pile is sometimes called flossa.

Plain weave The most basic weave formed by raising every even warp end over every odd weft shot and every odd end over every even shot. Also called tabby.

Ply A number of single threads that have been twisted together in a length of thread.

Quill A paper tube on which the weft is wound for insertion in a boat shuttle.

Raddle A toothed frame used to spread the warp while it is being beamed. Also called spreader.

Ratchet A wheel with notches or teeth, fastened to ends of warp and cloth beams to hold proper tension and to prevent unrolling.

Reed A comblike device set in the beater to space warp ends according to plan and to beat the weft down.

Reed hook A device with a hook at one end, used to pull the warp ends through the heddle eyes and reed dents.

Rising shed A shed opening made by the raising of alternate warp threads. (See **Jack loom.**)

Roving A soft, rope-like form of fibres from which yarns are made.

Rya A knotted rug with a long cut pile.

Selvedge Warpwise edge of the cloth.

Sett The number of warp ends per centimetre.

Shaft One set of heddles on the shaft sticks.

Shed The V-shaped opening formed by the raising or lowering of warp ends, through which passes the shuttle carrying the weft thread.

Shot See **Pick.**

Shuttle The instrument that carries the weft threads.

Singles One continuous length of twisted yarn that has been spun from fibres.

Sinking shed A shed opening made by the lowering of alternate warp threads. See **Counterbalanced loom.**

Skein Loosely wound yarn in a continuous strand. Also called hank.

Slabstock See **Back beam.**

Sleying Threading the warp through the dents in the reed.

Spinning Twisting of fibres to make a continuous strand of thread.

Tabby See **Plain weave.**

Take-up The contraction of yarn caused by the interlacing of warp and weft.

Tapestry beater A comb or fork used in a frame loom to beat down the weft.

Tension The degree of tightness to which the warp is stretched on the loom.

Tension stick A thin flat stick inserted into the warp in a frame loom to adjust the tension.

Tie-up The planned sequence in which the shafts are attached to the treadles of a floor loom.

Top castle The central main structure of the loom that supports the harness.

Treadles Foot pedals that are attached to the shafts on floor looms and raise or lower them.

Twill A basic weave in which the weft forms a diagonal pattern.

Warp The threads running lengthwise in a loom and through which the weft threads are passed to form the cloth.

Warp beam The rotating lower back beam around which the unwoven warp is wound and stored.

Warp-end bar The rod at the back of the frame loom around which a continuous warp is wound and spaced.

Warp ends See **Ends.**

Warp plan Indication of the threading order of the warp through the heddles. Also called drawing-in draft and threading draft.

Warping board Wooden frame with spaced pegs around which the warp is measured and wound.

Warping reel A large barrel-like revolving wheel around which the warp is measured and wound. Also called a warping drum.

Weave draft The draft that indicates the pattern of the weave.

Web Piece of woven cloth.

Weft The yarn that is interwoven with the warp ends. Also called filling.

Woof See **Weft.**

Further Reading

Fabric Structure

Advanced Textile Design: W. Watson, Longmans Green
Designing on the Loom: M. Kirby, Studio
Elementary Textile Design and Fabric Structure: John Read, Edward Arnold
Foundations of Fabric Structure: J. H. Strong, National Trade Press
Textile Design and Colour: W. Watson, Longmans Green

Hand Weaving Technique

Peter Collingwood — His Weaves & Weaving: Shuttlecraft of America, Monograph, 8
Designers Draw Loom: A. Hindson, Faber
Domestic Manufacturers Assistant in the Arts of Weaving & Dyeing: J. & R. Bronson, Branford
Hand Loom Weaving: L. Hooper, Pitman
Introducing Weaving: Phyl Shillinglaw, Batsford
Manual of Swedish Hand Weaving: Ulla Cyrus, Branford
The New Draw Loom: L. Hooper, Pitman
Treatise on the Art of Weaving: John Murphy, Blackie
The Weavers' Book: Harriet Tidwall, Macmillan, New York
Your Hand Weaving: E. Davenport, Sylvan Press

Hand Weaving and Patterns

Foot Power Loom Weaving: E. F. Worst, Bruce Publishing Company
How to Weave Linens: E. F. Worst, Bruce Publishing Company
Shuttlecraft Book of American Hand Weaving: M. M. Atwater, Macmillan
Swedish Weaving: edited by Thelma M. Nye, Batsford
The Weaver's Craft: Simpson and Weir, The Dryad Press

Pattern Books

A Handweaver's Pattern Book: M. Davidson, J. Spencer Inc
Hand Weaving Patterns from Finland: Pyysalo and Merisalo, Branford
Key to Weaving: M. Black, J. Spencer Inc
Swedish Handweaving: M. Selander, Studio
Weaving Patterns: M. Selander, Wezäta Forlag Goteburg

General Books and Allied Books

Anni Albers: on Design; Weslyan University Press
Anni Albers: on Weaving; Weslyan University Press
Ashley's Book of Knots: C. Ashley, Faber
Byways in Handweaving: M. Atwater, Macmillan
CIBA Review (libraries only)
Rug Weaving: Klares and Hutton, Batsford
Tappisserie de Jean Lurçat: Copyright of Pierre Vormes at Belvès
Your Yarn Dyeing: E. Davenport, Sylvan Press
Quarterly Journal of the Guild of Weavers, Spinners and Dyers

History

Ancient Decorative Textiles: V. Thurston, Favil Press
Historic Textile Fabrics: R. Glazier, Batsford
Man is a Weaver: E. C. Baity, Harrap
The Romance of French Weaving: Paul Rodier, Tudor Publishing Company
The Romance of Textiles: E. Lewis, Macmillan
Spinning and Weaving: S. E. Ellacott, Methuen

Raw Materials

British Pure-bred Sheep: National Sheep Breeders' Association
Fabrics for Needlework: R. P. Giles, Methuen
An Introduction to the Study of Spinning: W. E. Morton, Longmans Green
Sheep: J. F. H. Thomas, Faber
Pitmans Common Industries and Commodities Series
   Silk: L. Hooper
   Linen: Moore
   Wool: Hunter
   Worsted: Dumville and Kershaw
Your Hand Spinning: E. Davenport, Sylvan Press
British Man-made Fibres Federation, 58 Whitworth Street, Manchester
Cotton Board, The Royal Exchange, Manchester 2
International Wool Secretariat Publications, Dorland House, 18–20 Regent Street, SW1

Suppliers of equipment and materials

General Enquiries

Leisurecraft Centre,
Search Press Ltd.,
2-10 Jerdan Place,
LONDON, SW6 5PT

Dryad, Northgate, Leicester

The Hand Loom Centre, 59 Crest View Drive, Petts Wood, Kent. Callers welcome, but by appointment only.

Harris Looms, North Grove Road, Hawkhurst, Kent

Arrol Young, Netherdale, Galashiels, Scotland

Importers of Scandinavian equipment

Lervard (UK) Limited, 18 Vernon Buildings, Westbourne Street, High Wycombe, Bucks

Yarns

Craftsman's Mark Limited, Broadlands, Shortheath, Farnham, Surrey
(rug wools in natural colours, Welsh hand mule spun tweed and warp flax)

Dryad, Northgate, Leicester

The Hand Loom Weavers, Fourways, Rockford, Ringwood, Hampshire
(cottons)

Hugh Griffiths, Brookdale, Beckington, Bath, Somerset

T. M. Hunter, Sutherland Wool Mills, Brora, Sutherland
(tweed yarns)

J. Hyslop Bathgate & Company, Island Street, Galashiels, Scotland

Weavers Shop Limited, Wilton Royal Carpet Factory, Wilton, near Salisbury
(2 ply rug wools, and warp twine)

Ashford Spinning Wheel.

Other titles available in the Pan Craft Series:
FRAMING, MACRAMÉ, RUGMAKING, POTTERY and JEWELLERY